A HO

How-to-*do* books only tell you how someone else did something. They prescribe shortcuts for success. The methods explained may not work for you.

This book is a how-to-*be* book, a prerequisite for all the other how-to-*do* titles. In truth, author Tom Thiss has written an "Owner's Manual" for your life.

Most books will teach you how to make incremental improvements in the *content* of your life. This book deals with the *context* of your life and how you can make incredible, effective changes that give you true success and happiness. And that is really *how to be.*

In today's world, we all live in FUTURE SHOCK, as described almost
a quarter century ago by Toffler. Each of us needs to know
HOW TO BE at peace with ourselves and the universe.
This book provides a blueprint for your personal journey.
— *C. Norman Shealy, M.D., Ph.D.*
Founding President, American Holistic Medical Association

Tom's valuable lesson to us is that the only person you can truly change is
yourself, and by changing the way you communicate with others, you can
gain their commitment and support to achieve even the loftiest of goals.
— *George P. Julius, Jr.,*
President and CEO, Brooks Beverage Management

A masterful book in which Tom, through the Wizard, teaches us
to live life from the inside out. It's time that the book was written—
by a man whose writing is congruent with his living.
— *Ruth Stricker*
Founder/Director of The Marsh, A Center for Balance and Fitness

THE HOW-TO-BE BOOK

*A Fable with Exercises
to Take the Stress
Out of Your Life*

THOMAS THISS

DEACONESS PRESS
Minneapolis

To my brother, George, who never saw this book.

But if he had, we all would have been richer

for his wisdom, insight, and compassion.

Library of Congress Cataloging-in-Publication Data
Thiss, Thomas, 1929—
    The how to be book: a fable with exercises to take the stress out
of your life / by Thomas Thiss.
        p. cm.
    Includes bibliographical references.
    ISBN 0-925190-73-X
    1. Stress management.   I. Title.
RA785.T475   1994
155.9'042—dc20

93-49693
CIP

Published by Deaconess Press (a service of Riverside Medical Center, a division of Fairview Hospital and Healthcare Services, 2450 Riverside Avenue South, Minneapolis, MN 55454).

Cover/interior design by The Nancekivell Group.
Cover photograph by Tabor Harlow.
Author photograph by Jill Griffiths.
Chapter Two excerpts from The Fantasticks © 1964 by Tom Jones and Harvey Schmidt.

First Printing: February 1994.
Printed in the United States of America.

97 96 95 94 7 6 5 4 3 2 1

Publisher's Note: Deaconess Press publishes books and other materials related to the subjects of physical health, mental health, and chemical dependency. Its publications, including *The How-To-Be Book,* do not necessarily reflect the philosophy of Fairview Hospital and Healthcare Services or their treatment programs.

For a current catalog of Deaconess Press titles,
please call this Toll-Free Number: 1–800–544–8207.

ACKNOWLEDGEMENTS

This book had its origins in London, England. While living there from 1983–89, I commuted to the U. S. several times a year where I spent many weekends between consulting assignments writing early versions of this book.

In London, A. H. Abedi and John Hillbery gave me inspiration for much of the conceptual underpinnings of the text.

In the U. S., my colleagues at Organizational Resources International, Bob Alberts and Bob Spiewak, have been my loyal friends and co-facilitators in many seminars where these ideas were tested and refined.

Pat Samples gave me early editorial help of great value and pointed me to Jay Johnson, my editor at Deaconess Press who, more than anyone, has made this book a reality. Jay has been this book's most ardent champion and its most insightful critic. My thanks also to Ed Wedman at Deaconess whose great encouragement, and patience, made it all happen.

Rick and Jody Avery, Ralph Copleman, Anna Currence, Jim Gaughan, Dick Leider, Harrison Owen, Norm Shealy, and Ruth Stricker all read various versions of the unedited manuscript and gave me needed support and criticism.

My family has watched this evolve over a longer time

than any of us thought possible. My four boys—Eric, Ted, Peter, and Michael—were the subjects of many of my early management "experiments" at home. Through raising them, I learned more about management than from all the books I ever read. As young adults, they have been patient champions of this project, code named "The Wiz," as has my wife, Cokey.

The writings of several people had a strong influence on my thinking. Among them were Herbert Benson, Edward de Bono, Norman Cousins, Vaclav Havel, Hans Selye, and Carl Jung.

A special thanks to Chris Keeble for a great story, to Frank Beddor for his wonderful promotional help and to my parents, Chuck and Alice, who are both in their nineties and living examples of good stress management.

Lastly, I owe a measure of thanks to two long-deceased basset hounds, Douglas and Alphie, whose great stress-reduction capabilities gave me inspiration for two of the chapters in this book.

Tom Thiss
January 1994

TABLE OF CONTENTS

PREFACE

While living in London in the mid-1980s, I worked with an extraordinary visionary leader. He was an inexhaustible source of wisdom and inspiration. On one occasion while addressing a group of top-level managers, he said, "Don't be concerned about what you do. Pay attention first to what you are, and then bring those qualities into all that you do." That statement, exceedingly uncommon for a chief executive, struck me as profoundly wise. He was telling us to attend to our *being*. Today in America, we would say, "Get yourself together before you act." Although this book had many streams that gave rise to it, that one statement seemed to set its course.

I was repeatedly struck with my mentor's ability to move through a series of diverse encounters and approach each one focused and fully present. In a meeting he always took a few moments to center himself and to feel the energy in the setting before he began. He became the model for one of the main characters in this book, the Wizard of Is.

While living abroad, you often learn more about your own country than the one you are living in because you see America through the eyes of an ex-patriot. Often when entering the States after an extended time overseas, I would feel assaulted by the frenzied, stressful pace of life. It was as if everybody and everything were shouting at me. Soon, however, I would find myself swept up in the stream of events, a participant in the frenetic pace that had bothered me a short time before. It occurred to me that most people are not aware of this because they have not had sufficient exposure to anything different. They have accepted stressful lives not knowing they have other choices.

I knew that the global realignment process which was causing much dislocation in our country would continue, and the dizzying changes in our business marketplace would only accelerate. These changes we could do nothing about. The only stress-reducing option available to us, other than burning out or dropping out, seemed to be drawing on our deeper inner resources. Somehow, if we could bring the best of us to the moment we would neither be victims nor exploiters, but rather people with choices. Making these choices would be more a matter of using our internal resources than being victims of external forces over which we had little control.

A "how-to-be book" appealed to me because all the focus in our culture was on *doing* . . . and it appeared to me we weren't doing very well! We are *beings* by nature, but we have become "doings" by choice. The quality of those choices is directly related to our being, to who and what we are. It seems as if we have things backwards. Development is an inside-out process. It takes work. There are no shortcuts. As such, we need to know more about ourselves, our values, our talents, and our purpose for being. These existential issues need to be addressed if our lives are to be truly authentic. Otherwise, we are living lies.

I have been in the training and development business for over thirty years. During that time, I have taught courses or consulted in thirty-eight countries on six continents. In the last few years, I have seen remarkable changes. Many of those changes, however, we have been advocating for twenty-five years, and most are not happening as fast as they could. They are happening, however, because now they are economic necessities. A business changes when its life is threatened.

The same is true with individuals. I am continually amazed at what it takes to get people to change their ways. I believe this is so because most people are not in charge of their lives. They have turned that responsibility over to other authorities—corporations, money lenders, governing and political bodies, churches, medical groups, associations, peer groups, parent educators, etc. I hear it in statements like this: "I'd like to, but I've got two kids in college . . . ." or "I think you're right, but my boss . . . ." or "My doctor told me I had to . . . ." These authorities have huge vested interests in the status quo. The people representing these hugely influential interests make the big decisions for us, leaving us with only the cosmetic changes. The most important question we could ask ourselves is, "Who's in charge of me?" And if we are honest, most would not like to hear our own answers.

I have concluded that most of us have abdicated our priceless right of choice and we are really not aware that we are no longer in charge of our own lives. We think we are calling the shots, but the bigshots are calling the big shots! The loss of personal responsibility has been a gradual, erosive process. When made aware of this, however, the choice to set it right is ours. Nothing is more stressful than feeling that you no longer have control over your own life. This book is a twelve-part process for recovering that lost or threatened feeling. For you this choice may be so daunting that you opt to continue your life the way it has been. Governed by fixed habits, mindsets, thought patterns, beliefs, and perceptions that decide for you, you then unknowingly await a personal crisis. Only trauma can bring about needed changes.

If we were really in charge of ourselves, change would be simple and quick. We would run the proposed change by our value system and determine if the change were consonant with our purpose. If so, we would go with it. If not, it's a non-starter. To get to this point, however, we have a lot of work to do on ourselves. That's the inner journey the Wizard of Is talks about in this book. The journey starts either with curiosity or a crisis. For the vast majority, the latter does it for us. Life keeps giving us a wake-up call. The role of the Wizard in the book is to give readers a wake-up call, sounding the alarm of curiosity, not crisis.

The goal of traditional wisdom has always been to awaken to the truth. This truth is what each of us must seek for ourselves. One thing is certain: Truth comes from within, from the heart of our being. Discovering this truth is the most exciting journey ever undertaken, to a place where nobody has ever been before. The risk of not taking the inner journey is a life not truly lived. The reward of doing so is a life fulfilled. No risk, no reward. This book is a summons for all who wish to take the first steps to a less stressful and more exciting human beginning.

*The true perfection of man lies, not in
what man has, but in what man is.*
—Oscar Wilde

INTRODUCTION

In a busy, always-changing town in middle America lives
an unpretentious man. He is a doer of largely uncelebrat-
ed deeds of personal thoughtfulness. He lives simply and
he lives alone. Yet he is not, as you might expect, a lonely
man. Children love him. He attracts them like a Pied
Piper, delighting them with tales and with the treasures he
collects on his many travels. Above all other traits, this
man has a warm and welcoming way.

Perhaps what endears him most to the young people in
town is his message of *how to be*. He talks hopefully and
confidently of a better world, as if it were actually so . . .
and he makes a world that isn't always pleasant seem as
if it is. He speaks with an assuring certainty of a deeper
reality that lies behind what we see, the apparent. He
talks about the reality of what *is*. This is why the town's
children and their parents call him the "Wizard of Is."

There is mystery around the Wizard. When you are
with him, you feel calm, a sense of serenity that sets you
apart from the frenzy and uncertainty of the world. This
serenity causes the grown-ups in town to wonder, "What
does the Wizard know that we don't?" In times of stress
and change, it is hard to understand a man who helps
others feel inner assurance. But you *do* feel better when
you are with the Wizard.

Not much is known about his life, but rumors abound. Some people think he is a cult figure. Others just regard him as strange, and they keep a polite distance from him. The townspeople, by calling him the Wizard, sometimes conjure up questionable charges of mysticism and the supernatural against him. But these are unproven accusations, and the worst that could be said about the man is that he is *different*. This is precisely why children love him and some grown-ups regard him with suspicion. To many he symbolizes a threat to their lifestyles—after all, how can someone be so calm and confident when our society continues to feel the pressure to do more, to do it faster, and to do it with less.

The Wizard's prominence has grown in recent years. He has become a folk hero, a guru for searchers. This, too, has distressed some townspeople, as it has brought a stream of pilgrims into their small community and deepened their suspicion of strangers.

And one day I was able to witness this phenomenon firsthand, for I reached a time in my life—caught up with stress and personal concerns—when I felt compelled to visit the Wizard.

If you have come to me for answers,
then you have traveled in vain.

1

THE ANSWERS WITHIN

I first came to visit the Wizard when I was in my middle years. I was troubled and apprehensive, but eager to learn. The Wizard met me at the door, and he immediately offered me a cup of Tranquilitea, his favorite herbal tea blend. When I finished the tea, the Wizard asked me what I did for a living. I told him that I was a manager. With that, the Wizard smiled knowingly and asked, "Do you enjoy being a healer?"

Wondering if I had been misunderstood, I hesitated then replied uneasily, "A healer?"

"Why, yes," said the Wizard. He laid his hand gently on my shoulder. "You do not know you are in a healing profession? There are a lot of people who do their jobs and tend their homes every day, but they are living fragmented lives. Anyone who helps them put the pieces together is a healer. Healing is the process of becoming more whole, less fragmented. *Holy* comes from the same root word."

The Wizard stopped a moment, smiled at me again, then added with a nod, "I will wager you did not know you were in a *holy* profession!" With that we both laughed, and all my initial tension dissolved.

"I never thought of managing as a healing profession, let alone holy," I said. "If anyone needs healing, it's probably *me.*"

"That is precisely the point," affirmed the Wizard. "We cannot do much for others if we are not whole ourselves. Have you ever thought how much damage a 'sick' or fragmented doctor can do to his or her patients?

"*Iatrogenic* is a word that describes illness caused by a doctor's inappropriate diagnosis, manner, or treatment. The word *iatros* is Greek for *physician.* Iatrogenic illness is induced in a patient by a doctor's inept words and actions. It is very common, but probably no more common for doctors than for nurses, teachers, factory workers, parents, or any other profession. I call it 'managenic illness,' or problems people have that are caused by their managers."

"What kinds of problems?"

"Managenic problems are epidemic—low self-esteem, lack of confidence, dependency, guilt, anxiety, depression, fear and anger, just to name a few. *Stress,* with all of its physical consequences, is the big problem. Managing a business or a family is a huge responsibility. First, we have a job to do on ourselves before we can be of help to others. In this sense, we are all managers—managers of ourselves. It is a full-time job." The Wizard looked at me for a reaction.

"I guess that's why I'm here." I squirmed a bit in my chair. "I need help, and I'm looking for some answers," I said in my most businesslike manner.

"Have you come to find a cure for stress, a cure for the hurting we all experience?" asked the Wizard.

I was a bit taken aback by his reply. "Well, I'm not sure. I don't know if I need to be cured of anything."

"The word *cure* comes from the Latin *curare* meaning 'to take care of.' Are you looking for someone to take care of you?" the Wizard asked. He poured more tea into my cup.

"I'm quite capable of caring for myself."

"Good," replied the Wizard, softening his directness with a shrug of the shoulders. "Being in a holy profession, you should know that in the priesthood, *cura animarum* literally means the 'care of souls' or 'pastoral care.' The priesthood of management is no different. Good managers care for their people, and good parents care for their children, but they also need care. Let me rephrase my question. Have you come to me for pastoral care?"

"I guess so. All I know is, I've got problems and I came to you for answers," I said.

The Wizard reflected for a moment, and then spoke softly to me. He measured his words, as if to make each one count. "If you have come to me for answers, then you have traveled in vain. The answers you seek lie within you."

His words frustrated me. I quipped, "If they do, they haven't made themselves visible yet!" I laughed at my honest admission, and the Wizard joined in. "You know, I really haven't laughed much lately," I said. "It feels good."

"Laughter is one of the best healers," said the Wizard. "I call it 'aerobics for the spirit.' Laughing helps us maintain our mental fitness. As for the answers that have not yet revealed themselves to you, do not worry. Answers take time and patience. They are reticent by nature. We have to prepare ourselves to receive them, even to recognize them. It is almost always in a relaxed state when answers make themselves known to us, but they *will* come. Laughter helps prepare the way." I could tell the Wizard was pleased with my growing ease.

"Interesting that you should say that," I said, squinting my eyes and looking intently at my new mentor. "People always tell me I should try to relax more."

The Wizard shook his head. "Relax, yes. Try, no. Trying seldom helps you relax. That's like striving to sleep—it doesn't work. Relaxation is a natural, allowing process. Often we try too hard. Just *allow* yourself to relax. Your body knows how to do it, if you give it permission.

"The truth you seek to your everyday problems is really quite simple, but simple is seldom *easy*. An awareness of what lies within you is the key. When you tune into the inside, then the outside will take care of itself. Right now, you have access to all the power you need. Call it God, wisdom or intuition, if you will, but when you discover your inner power, you will have your answers. That is what *is*, and that is *how to be* in life."

There was a knock at the door, and the Wizard introduced me to two neighbor boys. They brought him a fistful of feathers, some spoor, a maiden hair fern, and assorted artifacts that they had just found in the woods. They knew "Mister Wizard" would tell them all about their discoveries, and he did.

SUGGESTIONS

The Wizard gave me some basics on stress management and then said I have, broadly speaking, only three choices for action:

BASICS:

* STRESS IS THE PHYSICAL CONSEQUENCE OF ANY DEMAND MADE ON THE BODY.

* MUCH OF OUR STRESS COMES FROM PROBLEM RELATIONSHIPS.

* IF THIS STRESS IS INTENSE AND PROLONGED, ILLNESSES WILL RESULT.

* THE TENDENCY IS TO BLAME THE STRESSORS, OR SOURCES OF STRESS.

* THE FACT IS, IT IS NOT WHAT HAPPENS TO YOU THAT HURTS YOU, BUT RATHER HOW YOU TAKE IT. IN OTHER WORDS, *YOUR ATTITUDE* IS THE KEY FACTOR.

CHOICES:

1. YOU MAY ADDRESS THE SITUATION, CONFRONT THE PERSON WHO IS THE STRESSOR IN YOUR LIFE. THIS REQUIRES ASSERTIVE, CARING ACTION. YOU SIMPLY DESCRIBE THE BEHAVIOR YOU FIND UNACCEPTABLE, PREFERABLY IMMEDIATELY AFTER IT HAPPENS, AND RELATE HOW IT MAKES YOU FEEL. AVOID MAKING JUDGEMENTS AND SUGGEST TO THE OTHER PERSON HOW YOU WISH TO BE TREATED IF THIS RELATIONSHIP IS TO GROW.

2. YOU MAY SEPARATE YOURSELF FROM THE OTHER PERSON. IF YOU CHOOSE THIS OPTION, DO SO JOYFULLY. SEPARATION WITH MALICE AND RECRIMINATION IS NOT AN ACCEPTABLE ALTERNATIVE.

3. YOU MAY CHOOSE TO LIVE WITH THE SITUATION. THIS REQUIRES ACCEPTANCE AND FORGIVENESS. THESE TWO CRITERIA ARE ESSENTIAL. WALLOWING IN MISERY IS NOT ACCEPTABLE. DR. NORM SHEALY CALLS THIS "GOING FOR SAINTHOOD."

Identify a relationship problem that you have, make your choice, and take the necessary action.

Your body will thank you for it.

*My role is to comfort the afflicted
and to afflict the comfortable.*

2

WHOLENESS, HEALING, AND HABITS

In the days that followed my first meeting with the Wizard I stayed in town at a small residential hotel. It was a week before I could see the Wizard again, and I nervously paced my room each night. Meeting the Wizard was so different from my daily routine that I felt a stranger to it all, yet at the same time, I was curiously attracted to the Wizard and his message. My mind was filled with conflicting thoughts and emotions. I didn't know what to make of it all. What I did know, however, was that I was drawn to a certain ineffable quality in the Wizard, and I wanted to experience more of it.

The meeting with the Wizard had already revealed something startlingly simple to me. I was one of those fragmented people the Wizard spoke about, and I desperately longed for a sense of wholeness. To that extent I did need healing, though I had never thought of my problems in that context before. I also was troubled by the thought that my ineffective words and actions had caused a lot of *managenic* problems for the people I supervised and for my family. Admittedly, I was stressed and I didn't have my act together, but I had always blamed it on the circumstances around me—my busy schedule, my workload, my health, the demands and responsibilities of my family.

In a few days it was clear to me why I had come to the Wizard. If I was to be a healer, I had some work to do on myself. It startled me that the people I manage and the members of my family look to me for healing. I felt over-whelmed and remembered the Wizard saying, "The answers you seek lie within you." I needed to hear more—a lot more.

The next time I had an appointment, I met with the Wizard in his garden. Leaning on his hoe and looking pleased to see me, he inquired, "Did you ever see the stage play, *The Fantasticks?*"

"No, I didn't."

"In the 1960s, it was the longest-running production in American theatrical history. One of the reasons for this, I believe, was its simplicity. There is a delightful duet about growing vegetables that Huck and Bell sing in the second act."

Using a small trowel as a baton and the garden as a stage, the Wizard strutted along the plant rows and addressed each plant in song:

> *Plant a radish, get a radish.*
> *Never any doubt.*
> *That's why I love vegetables;*
> *You know what you're about.*
>
> *Plant a turnip, get a turnip.*
> *Maybe you'll get two.*
> *That's why I love vegetables;*
> *You know that they'll come through!*
>
> *They're dependable!*
> *They're befriendable!*
> *They're the best pal a parent's ever known!*
> *While with children—*

It's bewilderin'
You don't know until the seed is nearly grown,
Just what you've sown.

So...
Plant a carrot,
Get a carrot,
Not a brussels sprout.
That's why I love vegetables;
You know what you're about!

"Encore! More!" I shouted, applauding.

The Wizard blushed, suddenly self-conscious about his exuberant performance. "Thank you. I've always enjoyed the lyrics and the music in that play. It was very popular during the turbulent sixties when parents didn't know what was happening to their children, to the social order, to their cherished traditions, and to themselves. It struck a chord somewhere deep within us."

The Wizard went back to his hoeing. "Gardening is a healing art," he said. "Do you enjoy gardening?"

"I'm not a gardener," I replied.

"If you manage people or raise a family, then you *are* a gardener."

"A gardener of people?"

"A gardener of *potential*. Belief in another person's potential is the most empowering thing you can do as a manager or a parent. Remember the Wizard of Oz? The Wizard gave courage, a heart, and wisdom to Dorothy's friends by merely affirming their potential. Gardeners and managers do the same thing. They both nurture potential.

"In nature, a seed is genetically programmed to become something. That something is already determined. Enfolded within the seed is the potential of *how to be*. Our job is to provide the appropriate context for it to unfold, to express that being, to release what *is*. It is really quite simple, my new friend, as simple as dragging this hoe through the dirt."

"But if everything was so easy, then I wouldn't be here," I said.

"Remember, simple is seldom easy. First you must take an inner journey of self-awareness to find out who you are." Placing his hands over his heart, the Wizard paused. Then he released his hands in an open gesture of giving. "Then you bring that sense of *how to be* into everything you do. That's what living is all about. Sadly, few people are willing to make that inner journey."

"You're really just telling me to find out what I do best and then do it," I said, in my most pragmatic manner.

The Wizard was hesitant. "Yes . . . for now that will have to do."

"You don't sound convinced."

"Like a plant that grows from a seed to full flower, there are stages in the evolution of our being. I am content that your understanding of what I am saying is sufficient for now. You are on an inner journey, or you would not be here, and you must take it simultaneously with the outer journey."

"There are two journeys?" I asked, somewhat puzzled.

"Yes. The outer journey is the visible one, how we live our lives. The reason for the inner one is to open ourselves up to the mystery of life, to give purpose and meaning to the outer journey. It is a journey to our being, a way to discover *how to be,* the essence of what we are. That's what *is*."

"I see where you get your nickname, the Wizard of Is."

"Potentially, we are all wizards because people, like plants, will *become* something with or without help. The difference is in the *quality* of that becoming. That is where managing a business or a family, like gardening, can make a difference."

"Quality!" I said, my face brightening. "Now that's a magic word in business today. And it's all about 'quality time' in parenting, too."

"I am talking about the *quality* of living an authentic, whole life. I am talking about developing what *is*, about being who you are," the Wizard said. "Just as the seed is qualitatively no less than the bud, and the bud is no less than the flower, the child is no less than the adult. Each is complete at a certain stage while still evolving to the next level. Even so, we are all incomplete in terms of our qualitative potential.

"The manager or the parent, like the gardener, must intervene to assist as needed in this natural process of growth. It is tough for seeds to germinate on barren soil or to break through an asphalt overlay, and it is difficult for people to grow when the conditions for qualitative growth are not present. Often, however, in spite of great handicaps, people prevail."

"Last time we talked about healing in terms of wholeness," I recalled. "I've thought a lot about it, and you're right. When a doctor heals, he makes us whole again."

"Doctors do not heal," replied the Wizard, gently but authoritatively.

"They don't?" I must have looked somewhat surprised.

"Doctors only *assist* the healing process. The same is true with the manager and the parent and the gardener," said the Wizard. "God heals. Nature heals. The body, mind, and spirit heal. Healing is a natural process and wholeness is the natural state. It is unnatural to be fragmented."

"I suppose you're right. I see now why they call you the Wizard!"

"I am glad I was not living in this country 300 years ago," observed the Wizard.

"Why's that?"

"Did you know that at the celebrated Salem, Massachusetts, witch trials in 1692, both women and men were put to death? And, of course, a male witch is called a wizard. This wizard stuff was risky business! Fortunately, times have changed, but it is curious how the two words have evolved—to be a witch today is still not considered positive by most people, but to be a wizard, or even a whiz—that is all very good."

"I certainly don't think of wizards and witches in the same context."

"Language influences us more than we realize." The Wizard was now in his element, the world of words. "Men often come out sounding better in the language of our male-dominated culture. When a man loses his sexual power, we say he is *impotent*. When the same condition happens to a woman, we say she is *frigid*. In using these words, society defines a man in terms of power and a woman in terms of temperature.* This means that men are supposed to be powerful and women are supposed to be warm. Why not warm men and powerful women?"

"I never thought of it that way," I admitted.

"Few people do. Our role as managers and parents," said the Wizard, "is to awaken others. If I have awakened something within you, then I am pleased. My role is to comfort the afflicted and to afflict the comfortable. Healing requires both."

I noted the impish grin on the Wizard's face. "What do you mean by 'afflicting the comfortable'?"

The Wizard picked up his pruning shears and gently snipped several small shoots off a young apple tree. Looking down at the shears in his hands, the Wizard said, "A doctor has many tools to facilitate the healing process. The harshest of these is the scalpel. It hurts when it cuts, but it is a healing instrument. Surgery, although it

*The Wizard is indebted to Sam Keen for this insight.

destroys, can expedite the healing process. As a gardener, we have to snip off some branches to give a tree shape and boost its growth. Sometimes as managers and parents we have to take 'surgical' action to change behavior.

"If you would like to understand what I mean by 'afflicting the comfortable,' it helps to know a bit about *habit*. Simply speaking, habits are patterns of behavior formed by our brain, the greatest patterning instrument ever devised. William James said that habits are 'the great flywheel of human behavior.' That metaphor illustrates the power of habit."

"Interesting," I said, puzzled. "I don't think of the brain as a habit-making device."

"The brain's most undervalued talent is its capacity to pattern," said the Wizard. "Patterns make things familiar and understandable for us. Without patterns, life would have no meaning."

"What kind of patterns?"

The Wizard tied up some errant sweet pea sprouts to a lattice of string. "The brain organizes the information it receives into patterns of perception that make sense to us. This is what makes things familiar. We then act on the basis of these perceptions. When our actions are repeated, they become habits or routines. The brain is at its uncreative best when it is acting habitually in its tried and proven ways."

"What do you mean by 'uncreative best'?"

"If the brain were not so brilliant in this ability to make things familiar to us, every experience we have would be new. Nothing would be familiar. Can you imagine what that would be like? You could not have found your way here today. You certainly would never find your way home. You would have no recollection of it, but it would not matter anyway—when you got home you would not recognize your own family!"

We both laughed at the absurdity of it all.

"And to think we take this all for granted," I said, throwing my arms in the air.

"Yes, that is why I say the brain is undervalued. We do not accord it the recognition it deserves. This brilliant ability, however, is also the brain's greatest limitation."

"How's that?"

"Habit patterns become routines, and routines become ruts. When life is a rut, we act without thought We become mindless, unaware, and out of touch with the present. We become trapped in a mindset. No longer mindful of the moment, we lose that special feeling of aliveness. Then we are, for all intents, dead."

"Dead?"

"Dead to the present, the only state in which we live," clarified the Wizard. "Therefore, dead to life. We exist, but we do not live. We are in our 'comfort zone,' a complacent satisfaction with things as they are. We are reluctant to try something new, to 'test our edges.' In a rapidly changing world, this can be fatal."

"So what are we to do?" I asked. "What can *I* do."

"We have to jar the brain out of its comfortable mindset, or life will jar it for us. We are often the last to realize when our habits no longer serve us well," explained the Wizard. "This is what I call 'afflicting the comfortable.' "

"But how can I jar my brain?"

"We have to jar our senses, jar our awareness, and jar our perception. In order to grow, we have to break out of these self-imposed, comfortable mindsets. This will heighten our awareness and put our senses on maximum alert. Then we will experience the feeling of aliveness once again." The Wizard opened his arms expansively and drew a deep, satisfying breath. "It's like going outside and breathing fresh air after being cooped up in a room for days."

"I need some of that fresh air, so how do I go about it?" I pressed.

"*Aliveness* comes from seeing and doing things differently. This is the essence of creativity. Creative artists see the world differently and interpret it through the media of paint, lyrics, music, photography, or dance. The enduring ones are those who change with the times. This is how they stay alive artistically. They have cultivated what Ellen Langer calls 'creative uncertainty,' and that enables them to stay tuned to the present. To keep breathing fresh air they must forever fend off the negative forces of habit."

"So now we're back to habit," I said with resignation in my voice.

"Remember," reminded the Wizard, "that's what the brain does best. The way we *see* things determines the way we *do* things. And the way we *do* things, in turn, influences how we *see* things. This forms a mindset, a closed habit loop of seeing things repeatedly in the same way and acting accordingly: If we always do what we always did, we'll always get what we always got. Breaking out of this mindset, or comfort zone, is difficult because it is uncomfortable. Habits persist unless we *afflict* our comfortable ways."

"How do you suggest we afflict ourselves?" I asked, rather fearful of the Wizard's possible answers.

"One way to set habits aside is to address old situations in new ways. A good method is to put yourself in unfamiliar situations. For example, traveling or living in a foreign culture will help you take a fresh look at your old ways. We do not have to go abroad, however, to find unfamiliar situations. Any new challenge will do. Start a new hobby, seek out new friends, take a different kind of vacation, do something daring . . ."

"Daring? Like what?"

"Last year for my birthday," the Wizard paused as he cocked his head to one side and shifted his eyes upward, "I went skydiving for the first time."

I went slackjawed. "Skydiving! What was it like?"

"I have never experienced a similar sense of aliveness. When you step out of an airplane two miles up, tumble out into space, and fall 7,000 feet in 35 seconds, you experience a sensory assault quite unlike anything you ever felt before."

"But why did you do it?"

"I wanted to test my edges. I was curious as to how I would react to the challenge. That is the 'creative uncertainty' I mentioned. In this sport, you really have to stay focused on the present. I had no idea how I would feel when the door opened at an altitude of 10,500 feet and the jumpmaster said, 'Let's go!' "

I looked at the Wizard with a mixture of awe and wonderment. "Skydiving is really quite safe, just unforgiving of mistakes." The Wizard chuckled. "At that height, you are approximately one minute from impact with the ground. That tends to focus your attention on the moment."

"I should think so," I exclaimed.

"But the point is, my friend, try to put yourself in unfamiliar situations. Another way to break habits is to enlarge the context in which you live and work. This is called *reframing*. The environmental slogan, 'Think Globally, Act Locally,' illustrates this. If we enlarge our frame of reference to think of the global consequences of our actions, we are likely to change the way we behave at the local level. Our reframed view may alter what we do. This is what we call the big picture. Seeing this larger view often afflicts our comfortable ways, however, and we do not make changes. We wait until things get intolerably bad before we break our habits. Then, like the alcoholic who loses a job and a family before taking treatment, we reluctantly change."

"I must be in one of those habit loops," I said with resignation. "My life is out of my control. I go from crisis to crisis. I'm not managing my staff very well. I'm not being a very good parent either. I'm just reacting to things, putting out the fires. It's very frustrating."

Holding up his index finger, the Wizard predicted, "If you make just one change, your work habits and your parenting habits will change significantly. I am talking about the need for you to understand the fundamental differences between *urgency* and *importance*."

"In my world," I retorted, "there is no difference. Everything is urgent and important."

"That is precisely the perception we will break, but that must wait until our next meeting. When you leave, I have something very important to do. There are some things I must plant before the ground freezes. Fall is nature's planting time. When we follow nature's plan, we are richly rewarded in the spring. That is the way life is."

SUGGESTIONS

Here are some of the things the Wizard had me do until our next meeting. I think they are helpful for you too:

* EXPERIMENT WITH YOUR ROUTINES BY CHANGING THEM. BEGIN BY FOCUSING ON ONE. CHANGE THE TIME, THE LOCATION, THE PEOPLE, THE DURATION, AND/OR THE AGENDA. OBSERVE WHAT HAPPENS TO YOUR LEVEL OF AWARENESS. LIKEWISE, OBSERVE WHAT HAPPENS TO YOUR ENERGY LEVEL.

* AT WORK, AT HOME OR AT PLAY, ADD AN UNFAMILIAR DIMENSION TO YOUR FAMILIAR PROCEDURES:

1. TAKE A DIFFERENT VACATION—AT A DIFFERENT PLACE, WITH DIFFERENT PEOPLE, OR AT A DIFFERENT TIME.

2. INVITE AN OUTSIDER TO A MEETING OF REGULAR INSIDERS.

3. DISCUSS A SUBJECT THAT ISN'T NORMALLY TALKED ABOUT.

4. ARRANGE THE CHAIRS IN A CIRCLE; REARRANGE THE FURNITURE.

5. LET SOMEONE ELSE MODERATE A MEETING YOU WOULD NORMALLY BE IN CHARGE OF.

6. FORM SELF-MANAGING WORK TEAMS.

7. ASK YOUR CHILDREN TO HELP YOU PREPARE SOMETHING NEW AND UNTRIED FOR DINNER.

8. LET THE CHILDREN CHOOSE A SUBJECT FOR FAMILY DISCUSSION AND RUN THE MEETING.

TALK ABOUT THE DISLOCATIONS, CHALLENGES, AND TENSIONS THESE CHANGES CAUSED, AS WELL AS THE POSITIVE OUTCOMES. WHAT DOES THIS SAY ABOUT YOU, THE PEOPLE YOU WORK WITH, OR THE OTHER MEMBERS OF YOUR FAMILY?

WHAT DOES THIS SAY ABOUT YOUR TOLERANCE, YOUR ADAPTABILITY, YOUR RESOURCEFULNESS?

* ASK "WHAT IF" QUESTIONS TO STIMULATE ANTICIPATORY THINKING:

1. WHAT IF YOU WERE GIVEN A FREE HAND TO DO WHAT YOU THOUGHT BEST FOR YOUR COMPANY?

2. WHAT IF YOU HAD A MAGIC WAND THAT ALLOWED YOU TO MAKE ONE CHANGE IN YOUR WORK LIFE AND ONE CHANGE IN YOUR FAMILY LIFE? WHAT WOULD THEY BE?

3. WHAT IF YOUR STAFF COULD FIRE YOU? WHAT CHANGES DO YOU THINK YOU WOULD HAVE TO MAKE?

4. WHAT IF YOUR CHILDREN COULD GIVE YOU A PERFORMANCE REVIEW? WHAT GRADE, A THROUGH F, WOULD THEY GIVE YOU, AND WHAT WOULD YOU DO DIFFERENTLY AS A RESULT?

5. WHAT IF YOUR BEST CUSTOMER GAVE YOU 30 DAYS TO IMPROVE SERVICE OR LOSE THE ACCOUNT?

6. WHAT IF YOUR MATE PUT YOU ON 30 DAY NOTICE? WHAT WOULD THE CHARGES BE AND WHAT WOULD YOU DO ABOUT THEM?

7. WHAT WOULD YOU DO DIFFERENTLY IF YOU COULD START YOUR CAREER OR YOUR FAMILY LIFE OVER AGAIN?

8. WHAT IF YOU HAD ONLY ONE YEAR TO LIVE?

9. WHAT IF YOU WON THE LOTTERY? HOW WOULD YOU SPEND $10 MILLION?

You can no longer be just a problem solver.
You must also become a possibility seeker.

3

MAKING THE IMPORTANT URGENT

In the days that followed, I tried to do some things differently. I left the Wizard's town and returned to the familiarity of my own city, my own job, and my own home and family. But I varied my route to work in the morning. Sometimes I took public transportation, which I had never done before. I altered my lunch time and I tried different restaurants and varied menus. I also changed some of my work routines. I switched a regular afternoon meeting to the morning, and I cut out other meetings altogether. These changes definitely enhanced my awareness level. Generally, I became conscious of spending more one-on-one time with my staff people. The thought of being a "gardener of potential" appealed to me.

At home I consciously made an effort to "afflict" my comfortable ways by breaking some of the patterns I had become accustomed to. I changed our menu for greater variety, took a more active interest in the children's schoolwork, planned some different family activities that focused on fun, and even shot some hoops with my son. I noticed an increase in energy as I shifted out of a habit pattern. Aware of all the new possibilities open to me, I felt totally alert. I seldom felt this way before, and I realized it was because my old habit pattern had obscured my perception. I knew how blinded I had become. How subtle those habit loops are, I thought to myself. Not knowing we're in the loops, we can't see our way out.

I now realized that the Wizard was right. The mind needs to be jarred out of its natural complacency. There is, however, dislocation and discontinuity before new routines can be established. But I was discovering that this discontinuity offered me the rich potential of creativity. I could fill that new void with anything I wished. Any number of possibilities existed. This awareness also gave me a renewed appreciation of the time-saving efficiency of a good routine.

All in all, my discoveries were an innervating experience, and I felt a new flush of aliveness. I could feel an urgency in my work and in my parenting, and I wanted to know how this *urgency* differed from *importance,* as the Wizard had suggested.

When we met again, the Wizard was in his garden. A month had passed and it was now autumn. I shared my excitement with him, especially about the increased level of awareness I experienced when I started new routines.

"Congratulations!" he said. "It takes courage to do what you did, and commitment. If you had been unwilling to try something different, you never would have felt that aliveness that comes from breaking new ground." With that, the Wizard made a sweeping gesture over the plowed ground of his garden plot.

"What you discovered was the challenge and excitement of *open space,* that time between the end of the old and the beginning of the new. Open space is a seedbed for creativity. We cannot be creative while locked into habit patterns. Breaking the habit enables us to fill the void with new initiatives. To gain control of our lives we have to relinquish control. It is one of life's great paradoxes."

"It sounds like double-talk to me," I said skeptically.

"On the contrary. It is really quite logical. In order to gain control of any situation with a new initiative, we have to surrender control of the old. This death of the old and birth of the new is the cycle of creation which creates open space in the interim. Traditional parents or business managers are not comfortable with open space. To them, unstructured time is unproductive time. They like to fill each moment with planned efforts. This, however, does not allow for the creative process to take place. Open space is essential for radical change."

"Radical change?" I struggled to mask my surprise.

The Wizard reached down and pulled out some large weeds from between the tomato plants. Working the roots free of the warm, moist soil, the Wizard held the fragile tendrils in his fingers.

"*Radical* is from the Latin word meaning *root,* so I am talking about change at the roots. If I tear out these tomatoes and then plant corn, that is a radical change. Radical change requires open space. To do that I have to 'let go' of my tomatoes and create an open space in which to sow my seed corn. It is the open space that makes the planting of seed corn possible."

I played back my understanding: "You're saying that open space is the fertile soil of change, and if I program my life too tightly, I will lose the potential for new directions in my life."

"You said it well," encouraged the Wizard. "Children need unstructured time to nurture their imagination and creative potential. This is the purpose of play. For adults, unstructured open space is our playtime. It is like open soil, and it provides the potential for radical change. As long as we have open space, we have potential in our lives. We can fill the space with any creative idea we choose. Once we fill that space, however, we commit ourselves to a new initiative which, like the corn, takes root as a new idea, a different routine."

"And once the new idea takes root, it's here to stay until we uproot it for something else. Right?" I asked. "Is change always a radical, uprooting process?"

"No, only radical change is uprooting. As long as we are committed to a new idea, we do not uproot it. We nurture it. This is what I did with the tomatoes a moment ago. I made it easier for them to grow by removing the weeds, not the tomatoes. This is change of a more gradual kind that supports and nurtures the existing idea; whereas radical change pulls up the idea by its roots, and replaces it with another. The optimal time to make significant change is when things are unsettled, like an unplanted garden. That is the fluid state of open space, the time to sow the seeds of our choice."

"The change may have been gradual for the tomatoes, but it was radical for the weeds!" I quipped with a mischievous smile.

The Wizard smiled back, enjoying my emerging playful manner. "Gradual change is the kind we make to improve an existing idea. For this process, we need a certain order and stability. The existing idea, pattern, or procedure in our lives provides this. But when the pattern breaks down, as it inevitably will, chaos and confusion set in. This is open space, the seedbed for radical change—the rich soil where a new pattern will grow. Leaders in the business community and innovative parents who understand this concept always use the uncertainty of chaos to make changes. Those who do not understand this process tend to impose controls which strangle the nascent change process."

"So we go from order to chaos and then back to order again," I summarized.

"That is exactly right. There is a time to pull up the

weeds around the plants, and a time to pull up the plants themselves. Knowing when to do one or when to do the other is an art."

The Wizard reached down and pulled a carrot out of the ground. Handing it to me, he smiled wryly and said, "Some managers uproot their people, and some parents uproot their children, to see how they are growing!"

I smiled. "I know. I've had that done to me."

"Yes," concluded the Wizard, "the chaos and uncertainty of open space offers the possibility of something new. Once we initiate the new, we enter a period of stability where we refine and improve our new order. In time, as this pattern ages and becomes increasingly less effective, we feel the need for radical change again. And so the cycle continues."

"It sounds like nature's cycle. Which reminds me—did you finish your fall planting?"

"Yes, thank you, I did. Nature blessed me with more time than usual. It has been unseasonably warm, as you know. The deep freeze has yet to come."

"Then your planting chores weren't as urgent as you expected."

"We must learn to create our own urgency on matters of importance. If we wait for situations to become urgent, we lose control of the situation and we eventually lose control of our lives. That is why we must take immediate action on things that are very important, even on those things that do not appear to be urgent."

The Wizard planted this seed with me during our last meeting. It was now time to germinate it. "Wizard, are you saying urgent is not important?"

"That is right, my friend. In fact, you could say they are opposites."

"That is hard for me to imagine," I said skeptically, folding my arms in a "prove-it-to-me" posture.

The Wizard smoothed out the fine topsoil in an open corner of his garden. He then took a stick and drew a line to form two columns. At the top of one he scratched a big "U" for Urgent, and in the other column he scratched a big "I" for Important.

"The distinction we make here will help you break the habit that everything is urgent. We will define *urgent* as immediate, a short-term crisis or problem. Whereas, *important* is significant, something that could really make a difference, a long term opportunity or possibility."

Then the Wizard scratched several words under the two letters:

<u>U</u>	<u>I</u>
immediate	*significant*
short-term	*long-term*
crisis/problem	*opportunity/possibility*

"In day-to-day life, the urgent and the routine drive out the important. After taking care of the routine and urgent matters, typically there is no time left for the important. This is the problem with crisis management for both businesses and families. It can only get us back to where we were before the crisis started. It does not move us forward. When we become exclusively problem solvers, we allow the urgency of events to dictate our priorities. We become consumed with crises, trampled by the march of events. In the words of one executive, we become 'fodder for time.'"

"You've just described my life," I admitted.

"The reason for this is simple," said the Wizard. "Problems are pushy. They are very aggressive, forcing themselves upon us. Possibilities are shy, and they must be sought out. It is like having two employees or two children—one named 'Problem' and the other 'Possibility.' The one is always intruding in our lives; the other is reticent, unobtrusive, scarcely noticed. Who takes up most of our time?"

"Problem," I answered, nodding my head knowingly.

"Imagine that you are at the office working with Peter Problem. He is taking up all of your time. Standing outside your door, unnoticed, is Paula Possibility, too shy to come in. Paula is patient, like all possibilities, waiting to be invited in. But nothing happens because of your preoccupation with Peter. Now Paula faces a choice. One option is to slip silently away, as most possibilities do. You as a manager will not be accountable for this unknown lost opportunity. But Paula can also lose her patience, burst into your office, and demand to be heard. In choosing this option, however, she is no longer a possibility. She is now Paula Problem, and her message is urgent. Now we have two problems, Peter *and* Paula. And, unlike possibilities, you will be held accountable for solving both of them."

"Paula Problem is like a phone ringing or a baby crying. Somebody has to pick it up." I could identify with this situation.

"That is right," acknowledged the Wizard, "but business managers and parents have become so enamored with problem solving that they have lost sight of possibilities. If your focus is only on problem solving, you will find yourself at the end of the year wondering where the time went and what you really have accomplished. Now you are a year older, more distressed, and you have little of substance to show for the time you have spent. Life has been a rescue and salvage operation, exhilarating at times, but ultimately exhausting. This is the road to professional and personal burnout."

"I can speak to that," I said, my shoulders sagging under a heavy weight. "So what can I do?"

"Become more creative," said the Wizard. "Only through a creative search for possibilities can you run your business without it running you, or run your family without it running you ragged! You can no longer be just a problem solver. You must also become a possibility seeker. Some people, of course, will always see problems. Significantly fewer will see the ever-present possibilities in all situations. The difference here is in attitude and perception, in how you look at life."

"I'm sure that's true, but why is it so?"

"I believe it has to do with the immediacy of problems. Problems are usually 'in-your-face' phenomena."

Intrigued, I asked, "When does a possibility become a problem?"

"For a possibility seeker, it never really does. If a problem is not picked up early, it simply presents itself as a 'late possibility.' It is an eleventh hour opportunity to do something that should have been done sooner."

"Aren't you just playing with words when you call a problem a late possibility?"

"It is much more than that," explained the Wizard. "Problem solving can only put us back on track. A 'late possibility' tells us we may still have time to lay some *new* track. In this sense, problems provide us with the opportunity to take us beyond where we left off. Every crisis is an opportunity. Every illness is a chance to be stronger and healthier than before. We have the capacity to position ourselves better for tomorrow as a result of every experience we face today."

"It's all in how you see things, isn't it?" I said. "It's the difference between getting back to normal versus being better than before. Normal could be getting back into the old rut again, couldn't it? So I can use any problem as a means or an opportunity to get me out of a rut, beyond where I am."

I could tell that the Wizard was pleased with my response. "It is all a matter of perception, as you said. Solving problems only restores us to our former ways. Possibilities, however, have the power to change our ways. They arouse us, uplift us, and offer hope. The power of possibilities is their ability to sustain us through the problems we face."

"We have to keep our problems in perspective, right?"

"Yes, keep them in the context of possibilities. Without possibilities, problems can be overpowering. And some problems will even diminish as you pursue possibilities. When you are working on the important things in your life, fewer crises will develop. In time you will gain control over the fragmented parts of your life and have more time to do the things you want to do."

"It makes so much sense. Why don't we do it more often?" I wondered.

"I will let you in on a secret," whispered the Wizard, drawing me closer. "We do not want to admit it but, in truth, most of us like things the way they are. Crises make the big decisions for us. They get the energy flowing and dictate where the time and attention go. Like autocratic managers or dictatorial parents, problems tell us what to do. In doing so, they spare us the difficulty of making tough choices."

"So letting problems set our priorities is a lazy way of running a business, a family, or a life. It's a cop-out."

"That is exactly right, my friend. Chasing after problems is an easy way you can avoid some difficult existential questions and some fundamental management and family decisions."

"So then what do I do?" I thought I knew the answer

but I wanted to hear it from the Wizard.

"So what do you do about the problems in your life? Try something simple. You can convert a possibility into a crisis. It is like inducing labor. You can precipitate a 'possibility crisis' on your own terms before a possibility goes away or becomes a problem. This is the only way a possibility can hope to compete with the immediacy of a crisis. You have to make the possibility more tangible and appealing, more exciting to attract the energies of those you wish to involve.

"The idea is to get people excited about a possibility and then to determine what must be done *now* if it is to become a reality. Then you take that first step with the same urgency that you address any crisis. That is a 'possibility crisis.' If it is not done now, we may lose the opportunity. That is what leadership is all about. Leaders are possibility precipitators. They empower us with the immediate presence of possibilities."

"What about managers?" I asked entreatingly.

"Oh, they are definitely more problem solvers than possibility precipitators."

"That's fascinating! Clearly, I've been more a manager than a leader. And I haven't been a very creative parent, either. You're saying I should take the initiative by precipitating a possibility of my own choice rather than responding to problems that force themselves upon me at work or at home."

"It is not a case of either/or." The Wizard was not limited to either/or thinking. "You will have to deal with both problems and possibilities, but it is a matter of balancing your priorities. Precipitating possibilities is a must, or you will never get long-term control over your life. While you are working within the realm of possibilities, you must deal with crises as they come. Problems are subordinated to the possibilities and, in time, they will diminish in number and intensity. This is how you can gain mastery over your work and home life. You must both lead and manage."

"I see I have a lot more to learn about this," I said, shaking my head.

"Only by focusing on possibilities can you break out of the gravitational pull of your problems. You have to think about potential to get beyond the present. Possibilities lurk in open space and offer the potential for quantum change."

"I'd really like to know more about how to find these possibilities."

As he had in our past meetings, the Wizard prepared me for the next stage. "It all begins with the images you carry around in your mind. These imaginative internal pictures usually dominate the images you receive from the outside world. A clear mental image of a desirable possibility is a compelling thing. If you desire something and visualize it very clearly, it is likely to happen. That is why it is very important to be aware of what is on your mind. We will talk about that another time if you wish to arrange another meeting, but right now my rose bushes need attention. I can see their possibilities, but if I wait much longer, I could have a problem on my hands."

The Wizard caressed the last fragile blooms of his rose bushes. "The growing season is short here, far too short. I do not like to see it come to an end, for these flowers give me so much joy. I know I will have to take some action now—getting these rose bushes pruned for winter—so I can experience their floral abundance again in the spring. That is the way life is."

SUGGESTIONS

The Wizard, once again, asked me to attempt a few exercises. Go ahead—try them for yourself:

* MAKE A LIST OF THINGS YOU WOULD LIKE TO DO THAT COULD REALLY MAKE A DIFFERENCE IN YOUR JOB, AND MAKE A SEPARATE LIST FOR YOUR FAMILY. ASSUME THAT ALL THE THINGS YOU ARE NOW DOING ARE ROUTINE OR PROBLEM-ORIENTED ISSUES. MAKE THESE YOUR LISTS OF EXCITING, NEW, AND FUN POSSIBILITIES.

* ASK YOURSELF WHICH OF THE ITEMS ON YOUR LISTS COULD HAVE A SIGNIFICANT LONG-TERM IMPACT ON YOUR BUSINESS OPERATION AND ON YOUR HOME LIFE.

* SELECT ONE OF THE POSSIBILITIES FROM EACH LIST. BREAK IT DOWN INTO STEPS. SEQUENCE THE STEPS, AND MAKE THE FIRST STEP A "POSSIBILITY CRISIS." NOW EXPERIMENT WITH THIS POSSIBILITY. TAKE REAL ACTION AND FOLLOW THROUGH WITH THE STEPS, BEGINNING WITH THE POSSIBILITY CRISIS. HERE IS AN EXAMPLE FROM THE HOME LIST:

ITEM:
SPEND MORE ONE-ON-ONE TIME WITH MY CHILDREN.

STEPS:
1. SET A WEEKLY SCHEDULE ON SUNDAY EVENING. BEGIN WITH A FOCUS ON TWO DAYS, TUESDAY AND THURSDAY.

2. COMMIT TO LEAVE WORK NO LATER THAN FIVE O'CLOCK ON THOSE DAYS.

3. BRING NO WORK HOME.

4. NEGOTIATE WITH EACH CHILD AN ARRANGEMENT WHEREBY IF HE OR SHE WILL DO SOME PREPARATORY WORK ON DINNER OR DO THE DISHES, YOU WILL MAKE TUESDAY DINNER THE EXCLUSIVE TIME TO DISCUSS ISSUES OF INTEREST TO HIM OR HER. REPEAT THE PROCESS WITH THE OTHER CHILD ON THURSDAY. IF THEY WISH PRIVATE TIME FOR SOME ISSUES, SUCH AS HOME WORK OR PERSONAL THINGS, TIME CAN BE ARRANGED AFTER DINNER.

5. DURING THESE PERIODS, TRADE-OFFS CAN BE MADE ON TV OR SOCIAL PRIVILEGES AS THE CHILD ASSUMES MORE RESPONSIBILITY.

6. PLAN ONE WEEKEND ACTIVITY DEVOTED EXCLUSIVELY TO EACH CHILD—A WALK, A SHOPPING TRIP, A SPORTING EVENT, ETC.

Do it now!

Make it happen!

Get on with it!

Ultimately, leaders do not possess visions;
visions possess them.

4

THE POWER OF POSSIBILITIES

I began to find immediate applications in my life for the distinction between what is urgent and what is important. I discovered that 95% of my time was spent in routine and urgent activities, like responding to demands imposed upon me by others at work, and putting out "fires" that might have been easily prevented. At home I found I spent much time monitoring disputes between my children. The Wizard was right. There was no time for the important things in my life. In the month that followed our last meeting, I discontinued several activities, I delegated others, and I continually asked himself the question; "Is what I'm doing the best use of my time right now?"

Here is just one example. I witnessed the empowering nature of possibilities as I counseled my staff on what they could do to impact our company in a significant way. An entrepreneurial spirit began to bloom as the important issues were being addressed and people began to feel they could "make a difference." In less than a month I had transformed the way I managed my business. The Wizard had predicted that this one change of perception would change my work habits significantly. Nothing I did on the job before had so dramatically changed things as this. I was also seeing positive changes in my family life as I changed my focus from problems to possibilities. In my excitement, I called the Wizard and asked if I could see him the following day. When I arrived, I found the Wizard sitting on his front porch.

"I'm so pleased I was able to see you on such short notice," I told him. "I didn't think you'd be available."

"I purposely keep open space on my calendar," replied the Wizard. "If you recall, that is fertile time. When I allow my day to be cluttered with busywork, I have no time for creative possibilities, and no time for you."

"Is helping me what you consider important?" I inquired timidly.

"Is it important to *you?*"

"Why, yes. Of course it is."

"Then it is important to me," said the Wizard. "Tell me, what have you discovered since we last met?"

"I discovered that I wasn't doing anything really important, so I had a team-building session with my subordinates, and we came up with a vision for our company." I spoke with pride. "We're now working on a set of objectives to carry it out. I can see a difference already."

"I am not surprised," rejoined the Wizard. "I would suggest, however, that you not use the word *subordinate*. We have talked about the powerful effect language has on us. If you label people as subordinate, they will become so. You want to empower them, not subordinate them. It is a useful word in the military, but is has no place in our vocabulary today."

"What do you suggest?" I asked, a bit surprised.

"Anything that does not limit them—people, colleagues, members, associates, partners, affiliates, staff, delegates . . . ." The Wizard raised his eyebrows and opened his palms as if to offer me my choice.

"They don't sound the same," I said.

"They are not the same. We are talking about a change of perception, and language can help us make that change. You will get used to using them, like using the word *vision*. Not long ago, vision was taboo in business. Now it is fashionable. Times change, and words change to reflect the times." said the Wizard.

"I guess you're right." I said. "Then the word *superior* is out, too?"

"Absolutely," the Wizard replied unequivocally. "That is a dreadful word! When the industrial revolution began and people flocked to the cities to work in factories, employers faced the problem of managing large numbers of people. The only model they had for management was the military, so they adopted its methods and its language. The military model outlived its usefulness long ago, but the methods and the language persist. Changing the language will help us change our methods."

"What model do we have to take its place?" I asked.

"*That* is the question," affirmed the Wizard. "We are in a transitional period where the old no longer works and the new is unfamiliar and ill-defined. I suspect there will be a variety of models to replace the old one. The terms 'superior/subordinate' indicate a rigid structural order. The old pyramid with its hierarchy of boxes, levels, and channels of communication is just too inflexible."

"But you have to have *some* structure." I was struggling with the possibilities here.

The Wizard placed his feet squarely on the porch floor and firmly gripped the arms of his rocker. Holding them for a moment, he then reached out with his knuckles and rapped sharply on the pillar beside him, as if to test its soundness. "To be sure, structure is vital, but it must serve us and not get in the way. Networks of individuals and teams are replacing the pyramid as the most effective means of communication. The CEO of the General

Electric Company says his objective is to create a 'boundaryless company.' "

"How do you control employees with a network or without boundaries?" I was genuinely puzzled.

"You do not control, nor do you want to. The *release* of energy, rather than its control, is the emphasis you want. In the information age, we have to access data quickly. Power lies in sharing, not withholding information. Leaders have a vision of what they want to accomplish, and they empower people throughout the network to make it happen. This provides a looser but more powerful form of control. Visions do not fit neatly into a tightly-controlled organization."

For me the questions were coming faster than the answers. "How's that?" I asked.

"Visions are commitments to the self to make something happen, but they cross functional boundaries, go well beyond job descriptions, and often exceed the authority given to the job. As such," said the Wizard, "traditional structures cannot cope with visions."

"So what can I do, Wizard, to change the structure of my business?"

"We need more fluid organizations and more open space so people can get on with their commitments. Networks of people creatively interacting serve this purpose perfectly. In organizations that encourage this, people find support they never knew existed. The organizational synergy is enormous."

My orderly world was crumbling all around me. I responded in the only way I knew. "It sounds chaotic."

"It is, and that is good. Creativity is chaotic. It is never neat and orderly. Have you ever visited an artist's studio? It is a disaster! Paint is everywhere. Some of it, the relevant colors and amounts, finds its way to the canvas, and somehow it all comes together. To the artist, the vision on her or his mind is as clear as the finished painting, but the open space between the image and the finished product is rather messy. The same is true for any creative endeavor. In business, however, it is not paint but ideas, energy, and information that is living and chaotic. Controlling that is like telling the artist what and how to paint."

As always, the Wizard was convincing. "That's a good analogy. You've made a strong point for vision. That's why I had that session with my subord— . . . with my *staff*," I said, correcting myself. "Perhaps you could help me understand this better."

"I would be happy to. *Vision* is such a misunderstood word. First of all, it is not something 'out there' or in the future." The Wizard pointed across the road, out past the dry corn stalks in a field, out to the horizon. Then, putting his finger to his head, he added, "It is in here, and it is happening now. It is a here-and-now, not a there-and-then, phenomenon. Vision is a living thing, and the more we think about it, the more it grows in clarity and intensity. This is what makes a leader powerful—the capacity to envision a desired state and to communicate it in a clear and compelling manner. Ultimately, leaders do not possess visions; visions possess them. This is how leaders make things happen."

The Wizard could not conceal an impish look. "It has been said that there are three kinds of people—those who make things happen, those who watch things happen, and those who do not know what happened!"

I laughed. "I regret that I am probably one of those people who don't know what's happened."

"And you are not alone," encouraged the Wizard. "The art lies in seeing possibilities, in seeing what you want. When you visualize something, you 'see' it in your mind's eye. You don't know where this is except that it lies beyond what you can literally see. As such, seeing possibilities is beyond the limitation of our senses. That is the power of imagination, my friend. You can imagine what you wish, unencumbered by conscious constraints. You can transcend your problems and soar into the realm of pure possibilities."

My face face lit up. "I just made a connection. In our last meeting, we talked about being possibility seekers. Imagination is the means by which we do so."

"You have just answered your own question, How do I become a possibility seeker?" said the Wizard. "You decide what you want, and then you imagine it to be so. You can become a possibility seeker by seeing the possibility in your mind's eye. Imagination makes the future happen now. Remember too, you energize the image by the act of imagining it. In other words, just thinking about it makes it more likely to happen. Focusing your mind empowers the object of your focus. This is the strength of concentration."

The Wizard began to pace back and forth with excitement. "A vision is a creative act. You have brought something into being. The artist has an image of what she wants to create before painting it on canvas, and the writer sees the plot unfolding in his mind before putting it on paper. This is the initial step in a sequence that translates image into reality. Vision is the start of a mysterious process that transforms dreams into reality. It is the link between mind and body, the first step in an action sequence powered by feelings."

"Powered by feelings?"

"Feelings empower," said the Wizard. "If you reflect on an event of the past, the feelings associated with that event come with it. Try it. Think back to a particularly satisfying moment in your life."

I remained silent for a moment, and then I slowly started to smile.

"You are enjoying yourself," observed the Wizard.

"I was thinking about when my son was born. That was the happiest moment in my life. I had always wanted a boy. While I was thinking about that event, I could actually feel some of the same sensations I experienced sixteen years ago." I cocked my head to one side in a reflective trance, glowing in silent remembrance.

The Wizard softly said, "You've made my point."

I looked up at the Wizard, and he continued. "A mental image of a past event summons the feelings that accompany it, as you have just demonstrated. Now remember this: The same is true when you project an image *forward*. For example, if you wish to be a more loving person, you simply have to imagine yourself so, and you will begin to feel more loving. The feelings will empower you to act towards others and towards yourself in a more loving manner. This may surprise you, but the mind does not know the difference between a vivid mental image and the real thing, something concrete and already manifested in your life."

"Wizard, are you saying that something in my head is the same as the real thing? I find that very hard to believe," I said skeptically.

"If the image and the feelings are vivid enough, then yes, your mental image is the same as physical reality. Tell me, when you see an attractive person on the street, does that person do something to you emotionally and physically?" asked the Wizard, zeroing in on my skepticism.

"Of course," I responded quickly. I didn't want to give the Wizard the impression that I was emotionally inert.

"Good. Now then, close your eyes and visualize that attractive person who stirs you emotionally. See yourself interacting together in a pleasurable setting. Feel the energy present—intellectual, physical, emotional. Observe the subtle ways that you find so attractive—the warm and affectionate eyes, the way the other person laughs, the spontaneity and natural manner. Notice how responsive that person is to your every movement. Savor the intimacy of the moment, just the two of you. Feel the . . ."

"Stop!" I said playfully. "I get the point. You had me in another world."

"On the contrary," said the Wizard, "you had yourself in another world!"

"Okay, I'm sold. Now tell me how I can use this wonderful visualizing power."

The Wizard stood up and walked into the house. A moment later he returned with a book of writings by Thomas Carlyle, the brilliant nineteenth century Scottish historian. The Wizard quoted Carlyle: "The thought is always the ancestor of the deed." Allowing a moment for the thought to sink in, he continued, "You recall when we recently met, we talked about perception and action. What you view or what you see in your mind determines what you do."

"But, Wizard, you also said the process works the other way as well. What I do effects the way I view things," I challenged.

"Yes, that is exactly right. Your experience will determine what you see and how you see it. That completes the loop—what you *see* determines what you *do,* and what you *do* determines what you *see.* You and most other people now go around in that loop, repeating your behavior mindlessly. If you wish to change your behavior, you have to change the images in your mind. It is simply a matter of choice, replacing the old image with a new one. *The thought is always the ancestor of the deed.* If you want to change your deeds, you have to change its ancestors, which are your thoughts."

"Is a change in thought really the only way out?"

"It is the only permanent way out," said the Wizard.

"You can break the cycle with a simple change of behavior, but it will be short-lived if the mental image does not change with it. Remember, it is the image you carry in your mind that tends to prevail over the images coming from the outside. All people see the world from the inside out. These mindsets, the habitual patterns we have set for ourselves, are difficult to break."

Repeating the Wizard's words from an earlier time, I said, "That is why we need to 'afflict the comfortable,' by jarring our perception."

"You remember well. Einstein said that we determine reality by the 'kingdom within us.' That is why it is important to know your inner orientations. Many of us are programmed with mindsets that prevent us from making new choices and creatively interacting with others. Some of these patterns date back to our childhood. The good news is that you have a choice. You can reprogram yourself. Anything that has been programmed into us can be deprogramed out of us. There is a simple way, but it will have to wait. In the meantime, if you practice visualization, you will not be disappointed. That is the way life is."

SUGGESTIONS

The thought is always ancestor of the deed. Start with these visualization exercises, and I think you'll begin to see your life change.

* HOLD SOMETHING IN FRONT OF YOU. LOOK AT THE OBJECT CAREFULLY. THEN CLOSE YOUR EYES, AND SEE IF YOU CAN RE-CREATE IT IN YOUR "MIND'S EYE." PRACTICE CLOSING YOUR EYES AND VISUALIZING THINGS NOT IN FRONT OF YOU.

* CLOSE YOUR EYES AND FOLLOW THE SAME MIND'S EYE RE-CREATION PROCESS FOR SOUNDS, SMELLS, TASTES, AND TOUCH. NOTICE IF YOU CAN RE-CREATE ALL THE SENSES EQUALLY WELL. WHICH IS YOUR DOMINANT SENSE? THE VISUAL SENSE IS DOMINANT FOR MOST OF US. WORK WITH YOUR LESS DOMINANT SENSES AS WELL AS YOUR DOMINANT ONE TO BROADEN YOUR RANGE OF IMAGING.

* CLOSE YOUR EYES, AND SEE YOURSELF DOING SOMETHING THAT YOU REALLY WANT TO DO. SEE YOURSELF DOING IT PERFECTLY. IF YOU HAVE DIFFICULTY SEEING YOURSELF DOING IT, VISUALIZE SOMEONE WHO DOES IT WELL. THEN REPLACE THAT IMAGE WITH YOURSELF. WHEN YOU CAN SEE YOURSELF DOING THIS AND YOU CAN FEEL THE PULL TOWARD DOING IT, YOU MAY BEGIN PHYSICALLY TO TAKE THE STEPS TO MAKE IT HAPPEN.

* VISUALIZE A PROJECT IN ITS COMPLETED STATE. SEE IT NOW IN YOUR MIND'S EYE AS YOU WOULD LIKE IT TO BE. FEEL THE SATISFACTION OF ITS COMPLETION AND FEEL THE DESIRABILITY OF ITS ACCOMPLISHMENT. REPEAT THE VISUALIZATION AND FEELING PROCESS AS OFTEN AS YOU WISH. SAVOR THE JOY OF THIS POSSIBILITY. ALLOW THE GOOD FEELINGS OF THIS IMAGE TO MOTIVATE YOU TO ACT ON IT. KEEP THE VISION CLEARLY IN MIND TO CARRY YOU THROUGH ANY OBSTACLE YOU MIGHT ENCOUNTER.

Believe in the possibility!

The truth is that you energize what you think about.
You empower what you attend to.

5

IMAGINATION—
THE NEW REALITY

For the next several weeks I was obsessed with my new insights on vision. To me, vision had only been a fancy word for long-range planning, like determining management objectives at work or saving money for my children's college tuition. Vision was always dressed up a little bit so it could be framed and hung on the walls as executive boilerplate—something that nobody could disagree with or get excited about.

Now vision had become a living thing. I vividly recalled how the Wizard had demonstrated through mental imagery that the mind and the body are one. The link between thoughts and feelings is very real in the recollection of past events. This certainly was not a new idea, but somehow I had never realized how it could be consciously applied to my future. I saw the possibilities of the future and the present becoming one with imagination. I was practicing pure alchemy, transmuting baser metals into gold!

I was also eager to see the Wizard again and learn the simple way to visualize and change mindsets. When the Wizard and I met again, he invited me to take a walk behind his house. We strolled through a wooded area of maple, oak, birch, and some Norway pine. We walked silently for some minutes when the Wizard paused and, seeing a fallen birch, peeled off a small strip of its white outer bark. Taking a pen from his pocket, he drew a circle on the birch bark.

"You will recall the habit loop, the mindset, that began with perception—what you see determines what you do." He wrote the word *Image* at the top of his circle. "All perception is imagery, mental imagery. Everything you see is an image in your brain. In that sense, all reality is imagery to you."

"You're saying it all starts with imagery," I repeated.

"Yes," said the Wizard as he moved his pen clockwise on the circle, writing the words *Feeling* and *Action* to form a three-step process. "The image is the key because it evokes the behavioral process that follows—an image arouses feelings, feelings precipitate action, and action reinforces the image.

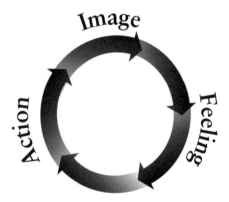

"All conscious acts begin with an image. Feeling and action convert that image into reality. And a vision is an image in here." The Wizard pointed to his head.

"Having the vision inside you links your future with your present. When you visualize something, it becomes real to your mind—*now.* In other words, in your mind's eye it is actually happening. In effect, you have fooled the mind into thinking it is occurring because it does not know the difference between vivid imagery and the actual happening. Once your mind grasps that desirable vision and actually sees it happening, it is hard for it to let go. That vision creates compelling commitment, and you find yourself drawn inexorably toward the new reality in your mind. It is powerful stuff."

"I see what you mean," I said. "You're getting charged up just by talking about it."

The Wizard excitedly continued. "Have you ever imagined something and said, 'It was so real I could see it happening'? Vivid mental imagery employs all the senses. This reveals another secret: Thinking about possibilities generates more excitement than thinking about problems. The energizing nature of possibilities enables you to surmount your problems. Without a vision, your problems can become overwhelming, my friend. With a vision, your problems become merely nettlesome obstacles. The Book of Proverbs says, 'Where there is no vision, the people perish.' The same could be said of today's business and family life."

"Aren't you just talking about visionary leaders, charismatic types—the few that have this talent?" I asked.

"Surely this gift is well developed in extraordinary businesspeople and in superparents, but all of us have this capability. You may recall I said that belief in another's potential is an empowering act. When you believe in people, you will help them become more responsible for themselves. They will feel encouraged to take charge of their own lives and rise above the problems they face. It is true for associates at work. It is also true for people in personal relationships with you, from significant others to children. This is the message in *The Wizard of Oz.* The

Tin Man, the Scarecrow, and the Cowardly Lion all felt empowered with the gifts they received: a heart, a brain, and courage.

"The sporting world is filled with stories of coaches who empowered doubting athletes to reach performance potentials previously unknown to them. The same is true in the world of medicine. Doctors often encourage patients to use the formidable powers of their minds to rise above their afflictions."

"So why should we expect less from the business world?" I asked. "And why can't we use the same principles at home, too?"

"Exactly. A friend of mine wanted to remodel his house. Four builders were asked to bid. Three saw nothing but problems. The fourth laid out several exciting possibilities. When my friend asked him how he was able to come up with so many ideas, he replied, 'I see beyond the walls.' Asked what he meant by that statement, the builder pointed outside to some shrubbery obscured by a wall. 'Those bushes are too lovely to sit out there unseen. I imagine how they would look from your living room, without the walls. I see beyond the walls.'

"With mental imagery, you can see 'beyond the walls' to the possibilities that lie ahead. You can break out of what William Blake called your 'mind-forged manacles' and see the possibilities unfold before you."

"Very interesting," I said. "I'm beginning to see some connections. Last time we met, you asked me to become a 'possibility seeker.' Now you're saying that mental imagery and feelings convert these possibilities into action. This three-step process takes us 'beyond the walls' imposed by problems. Presumably the vision is attractive enough to carry us through the problems. Without the vision, we could lose the will to continue. Right?"

Looking rather pleased, the Wizard smiled. "I could

not have said it better. Mental imagery brings the future to life within you right now. This starts a process that translates the image into reality. When an image in your mind becomes real to you, it becomes your 'new reality.' You have seen something better and you are no longer satisfied with the old reality, the way things are. It is this dynamic that literally pulls you out of the comfort zone of the old way, pulling you into the new reality of possibilities. Pierre Currie said, 'It is necessary to make life a dream, and of that dream, a reality.' That says it all."

"The future becomes the present by my ability to imagine something as if it were so," I echoed. "But surely you're not saying that all I have to do to make something happen is to just see it in my mind's eye."

"Of course not. But this is the first step, and without taking it, it is very unlikely that anything will happen. The truth is that you energize what you think about. You empower what you attend to. Action follows mental imagery. And when you use your imagination, you receive a very special bonus."

"What's that?"

"Imagery activates the right hemisphere of the brain, which is closely linked with the unconscious mind. With the image clearly and vividly in mind, you can program the unconscious to help you attain what you have in mind. This is an awesome force to have as an ally. The unconscious is where habits are stored. Through imagery you literally reprogram your unconscious mind with new habits to help you get what you want. Things that people attribute to luck, good fortune, coincidence, or synchronicity are often the work of the unconscious mind selecting and screening inputs to the conscious mind."

"I think I know what you mean," I said hesitantly. "A friend of mine is a naturalist. He finds wildlife where no one else can, probably because he has conditioned his mind to seek it out. Nature's clues are there for all to see, but they are noticed only by those whose minds are trained to see them."

The Wizard reached down beside the path. Brushing aside the larger fronds of an ostrich fern, he found a wild raspberry bush sheltered beneath it. Gently he removed a berry and handed it to me.

"How did you know it was there?" I asked.

"Just as you said before, I have trained myself to see these things."

"I remember the first time I bought tires for my car," I reminisced. "I thought I was lucky to find an ad for tires on sale. Later, I realized tires are *always* on sale. I had never noticed the ads until I needed tires."

"Need has a wonderful way of focusing the mind," said the Wizard.

"I know what you mean. Last year, I had to give a talk on a subject I knew little about. In preparing for it, information came to me from sources I never expected. At the time, I thought it was a remarkable coincidence. In hindsight, I can now see how the unconscious mind alerted me to images that would normally have gone unnoticed."

"Yes, mental imagery, with the help of a trained unconscious mind, gets you 'beyond the walls' of your limiting or negative mindsets."

"If I think of negative things, do I strengthen them as well?" I wondered.

"To be sure," replied the Wizard. "The negative things in your life are the walls. You can redirect negativity with positive imagery." With that, the Wizard stopped on the wooded pathway. He turned toward me with the birch bark still in his hand, and he wrote the word *Negative* in front of each of the three words on the circle: *Negative* Image, *Negative* Feeling, *Negative* Action.

"If I do not see myself as capable of giving a speech,

then the mere thought of it terrifies me. It raises my stress level and floods me with feelings of fear and inadequacy, making it nearly impossible for me to speak effectively. This state of distress is commonly called 'stage fright.' Some say it is our number one fear, death being farther down on the list. Many people would rather die than give a speech!"

I laughed. "I *know*. I can identify with that."

"Well, you can conquer stage fright in a simple way. The cycle can be broken at two places." Again, the Wizard pointed to the circle he had drawn on the bark, and he scratched out the word *Negative*. "First, break the cycle at the image stage simply by redirecting your energy from worrying to a positive image. All you have to do is to see yourself performing successfully. See the audience responding positively and feel the euphoria of the moment. Imagine the people coming up to you after-wards and saying how much they enjoyed your talk. This will arrest the worry and start the energy moving toward a positive experience."

With that, the Wizard scratched off the remaining two negatives and said, "Positive mental imagery transforms and redirects negative energy."

Having had some unpleasant speaking experiences, I was still doubtful. "I find it hard to believe it's that easy."

"I never said it was *easy*. The process is simple, but simple is seldom easy." The Wizard had repeatedly made this point. "Even the doubts you express now will erode the process. The image in your mind of a speech with a wonderful outcome must be very desirable, very com-pelling. Then it will begin to unfold."

"You said there were two places where the negative cycle could be broken," I reminded the Wizard.

"Yes. The second place to break the negative cycle is at the action stage. You give a great speech simply by acting 'as if' you were a great speaker. In California, they say you 'fake it 'til you make it.' It is a well-known acting principle. The late Cary Grant, perhaps the most loved actor of his time, said he was successful because he pretended to be someone he wanted to be until he became that person. Act and you shall become. What you are really doing is selling yourself."

"Selling myself?"

"Effective salespeople do not sell products, they help the buyer imagine satisfaction. People buy products that they imagine will make them more comfortable, more secure, more desirable, more confident—whatever they would like themselves to be. When they link this image in their minds to the product, they buy. Technically speaking, they sell themselves.

"The process of creating mental imagery is a buying cycle. When you imagine something you want, you are 'buying in' to a new image, an image of a better you, a better life, or a better world. After creating these images of satisfaction, the salesperson then acts 'as if' the other has bought. This positive expectation contributes to a positive outcome. When you do not have a salesperson to help you imagine, you can go through the process yourself. That's why I say that creating mental imagery is really selling yourself. It is a time-tested process."

I realized that what the Wizard was talking about had just happened to me. I had just 'bought in.' "It's really pretty simple, isn't it? Do you have any suggestions on how I can start the whole process?"

"An easy way to begin," said the Wizard, "is with *affirmations*. An affirmation is simply a statement you make to yourself that affirms the image. With affirmations, you can talk to yourself using words to describe the image. This 'self-talk' affirms the future outcome, as if it were already so. Positive mental imagery and affirmations are powerful forces for change. Images activate the right hemisphere of the brain. Affirmations activate the left, or language side. Together, images and affirmations enlist the powers of the whole brain."

"So what I say to myself is just as important as what I image," I said.

"The outcome is best when they work together. Often, however, your self-talk is negative and works against the positive imagery, or your talk is positive but you cannot see anything good happening. Positive self-talk is needed to affirm the imagination, to put the image into words. For example, if you wish to be more assertive, you simply state the affirmation as if it were so, and you visualize it simultaneously: I am an assertive person, or People appreciate my assertive manner.

Affirmations are short, specific, positive, and always in the present tense. Simply say as you see it. Your purpose in using them is to offset everything negative and to embed in your mind the positive image you wish to create. When the image becomes vividly clear and compellingly desirable, then you will be moved to taking action. You will have empowered an image and brought it into being. That is action a business manager and a busy parent can understand," he said, smiling at me. "Speaking of action, are you an aerobic-walker?"

"I'm not sure what you mean by that." I was a bit fearful of what I might be asked to do.

"Right now, I feel the need to quicken the pace, to raise my heart rate a bit. When I do this, I imagine I am a world-class walker. Come with me, and I will show you how to do it." With that, the Wizard set out briskly on the path. He grinned back at me and, bending his arms at the elbows, he began pumping them vigorously and forged ahead with a sudden burst of speed.

SUGGESTIONS

And so I began to combine positive affirmations with mental imagery. The following guidelines will be useful as you prepare and use your own positive affirmations:

* CREATE AS MANY AFFIRMATIONS AS YOU WISH. BEGIN WITH ONE TO START THE PROCESS.

* WRITE THE AFFIRMATION DOWN AND REPEAT IT AS OFTEN AS YOU WISH.

* THE BEST TIMES TO CONCENTRATE ON YOUR AFFIRMATION ARE IN MOMENTS OF RELAXED AWARENESS, DURING QUIET TIMES OF REFLECTION.

* WHEN REPEATING YOUR AFFIRMATION, REFLECT ON ITS MEANING AND EXPERIENCE THE FEELINGS IT INDUCES. VISUALIZE YOURSELF EXPERIENCING THE DESIRED STATE.

* REMOVE ALL DOUBT IN YOUR MIND.

* SPEND AS MUCH TIME ON YOUR AFFIRMATION AS YOUR CONCENTRATION ALLOWS. A FEW MOMENTS MAY BE AMPLE.

* IF YOU WISH, YOU MAY BEGIN THE AFFIRMATION PROCESS WITH THE SERENITY PRAYER:

God grant me the serenity to accept the things I cannot change;
The courage to change the things I can;
And the wisdom to know the difference.

(YOU MAY SAY "GRANTS" TO KEEP THE PRAYER IN THE PRESENT TENSE.)

SUMMARY:

If you see it as if it were so, and
you feel it as if it were so, and
you act as if it were so, and
you say it as if it were so . . .
then it is more likely to be so.

The first priority of a manager is people development,
and the means to do so is work.

6

GETTING OURSELVES TOGETHER

During the next few weeks, I thought a lot about imagery. The Wizard's story about going "beyond the walls" had new meaning for me. I realized that I was the wall. There were several times when I caught myself thinking of all the reasons why something couldn't be done. I now consciously arrested these thoughts and began to look beyond the problems and think about how it could be done. I found that my mood changed as my thoughts changed. I proved to myself that images give rise to feelings and actions, and what we have in our minds is the determining factor. A new sense of power came over me as I thought about all the possibilities this suggested.

I also noticed that if I imagined the potential of my office staff or my family members, my relationship with them changed. I saw them all as having greater value, and they in turn responded to my positive expectation. What the Wizard said was true. When I attend to the image I have in my mind, I bring that potential into being. What extraordinary powers we have that we don't even begin to use! I couldn't wait to share the excitement of these newly-found powers with the Wizard.

When we next met, the Wizard was organizing a trea-

THE HOW-TO-BE BOOK

sure hunt with neighborhood children. "It is a pity adults
do not have this much fun at work. Children are natural
practitioners of the art of being alive. They develop
through play, which is a child's work. Adults develop
through work, which should be our form of play. This is
what management is all about—getting people *done*
through work."

"Getting people *done* through work? What do you
mean by that?"

At that moment, several children ran up to the Wizard
to ask him to identify what they had found—pinecones,
feathers, wild flowers, seeds, leaves, and bark. If they
were not objects needed for the treasure hunt, they
dropped them immediately and rushed back into the
woods to search again. The Wizard seemed to draw energy from the enthusiasm of the children. They were so
open, so focused, and having so much fun. The Wizard
said it was because children had no mindsets.

The Wizard stepped away from the game to answer my
question. "The classic definition of *management* is 'getting work done through people,' but that has the wrong
emphasis. Business must strive for both work completion
and people development. It is a matter of which comes
first. Most managers have work completion as their first
priority . . . but because people do the work, they must
come first. The first priority of a manager is people development, and the means to do so is through work. That is
why I say management is the art of getting people *done*
through work."

I gave the Wizard a look of mild amazement. "You
always see things a little differently, don't you?"

"That is what creativity is all about—different perceptions. Seeing things differently keeps you out of those
insidious mindsets, those self-perpetuating habit loops.
Speaking of habits, how have you been doing on imagery

and affirmations?" probed the Wizard.

"I really could sense the power of imagination, but I felt rather silly saying those positive things to myself that weren't actually so," I said, embarrassed.

"Anything new seems strange at first. But please realize you do not have any difficulty saying negative affirmations to yourself such as 'I can't do that' or 'That's not my style' or 'I just can't see myself in that situation.' These are no more real than the positive statements you have trouble saying, yet you have convinced yourself that the negative ones are so. By affirming the negative, you restrict yourself to a comfortable but limited mindset, and you feel insecure when circumstance forces you out. Affirmations are one way to break out, but you have to believe them. Otherwise the process is merely mechanical, and it will not work. It sounds as if you have doubts." The Wizard invited my response.

After a brief pause, I raised my eyes and said, "I guess I do. Any suggestions?"

"Always!" The Wizard was never short on suggestions. "The key to change is *awareness,* relaxed awareness. Another name for this is *concentration."*

"I'd like to know more about that. I have trouble concentrating," I admitted.

The Wizard began, "There is a quiet time associated with growth and development. It is a time to get yourself together, to sort yourself out, to open yourself to the energy within and around you, to unify your mind and body. Experience shows that the calmer you are, the more access you have to your creative or intuitive powers. This is not thinking time, my friend. It is time to quiet the thinking mind and allow the unconscious mind to work its integrating ways. Imagery and affirmations work best in a quiet, reflective, meditative, prayerful state—a state of relaxed awareness."

"A lot of people like me are wound-up most of the time, and we find it hard to wind ourselves down to this state," I complained. "It's hard to convince people like me that this is a useful activity when a situation cries out for decisions and action. It could be an unhappy client demanding satisfaction or one of my kids testing the limits of my authority."

"The late Joseph Campbell, a mythologist, said, 'An athlete in championship form has a quiet place in himself. It's out of that that his actions come. If he's all in the action field, he's not performing properly.' "

Then with a playful smile, the Wizard said, "An English friend of mine calls this non-stop action 'mindless self-propulsion.' "

I responded with a sense of resignation. "I spend a lot of time mindlessly propelling myself."

"Many business managers never come close to their potential for this very reason. The quiet place in oneself is a preparatory stage for action. Here you heighten and focus your concentration powers. You bring your whole self together into the act. You summon your innermost resources to make your action more powerful and purposeful. The process begins with the physical centering of the body. Have you ever started an activity and found yourself out of rhythm and unable to recover without stopping and starting over?"

I laughed, knowingly. "That happened to me just the other day when I was giving a presentation to my board of directors. I got started wrong and I never did recover. Where were you when I needed you?"

"This happens when you start anything uncentered," acknowledged the Wizard. "Watch a diver before she begins her approach on the board. Notice a gymnast as he mentally prepares himself for his floor routine. They are getting themselves together in *stillness* so they may summon all their powers for their brief test of athletic and artistic skills."

A smile crept across my face. "You're saying that if I had approached my board with the same centered concentration that the diver approached her board, I wouldn't have had any problems."

The Wizard answered with a smile. "Nice play on words. And you are exactly right. We can learn much from athletes and performing artists. Their success depends largely upon their ability to retain this inner calm of relaxed awareness throughout their performance. The dancer, Jean Erdman, says there is a center out of which you act. That center has to be known and held."

"So this quiet center is not just a preparatory stage— it's a continuing thing as well." I felt I was becoming an accomplished active listener.

"The conscious mind cannot possibly control all the complex moves in these supreme tests of skill. Athletes must rely on their bodies, and a wisdom that comes from years of disciplined practice and a relaxed, open awareness to feeling feedback. William Blake said, 'Mechanical excellence is the vehicle for genius.' Genius only comes when you have mastered the mechanics of a discipline. Then when your mind is open to feedback from your body, it will teach itself. Tim Gallwey and Bob Kriegel, authors of *The Inner Game of Skiing,* say 'If the body knows, let it happen. If it doesn't, let it learn.' " The Wizard paused to give me some space.

"And you say this is not a conscious thinking process?" I questioned, cocking my head doubtfully.

"Absolutely not! The time for thinking is before and after you take action, but not during. Gallwey and Kriegel say you have to be 'extraordinarily sensitive to feel.' Skiing is too fast and the skills are too complex for the rational thought process. These examples are of ath-

letes acting alone, but think how complex the skills
become when you are on a team competing with others.
The need for centering is all the greater. The same is true
in all forms of human interaction, not just competition."

"I can see that," I exclaimed. "When the diver and the
gymnast center themselves physically, they also are centering their minds as well, aren't they?"

"As the British say, you are *spot on*," affirmed the
Wizard. "You cannot separate the two. The mind and the
body are one, so when you alter the mind, you alter the
body. You have to take that inner journey first to make
the outer journey more focused."

"So the inner journey centers me to make the outer
more powerful and purposeful." These brief summaries
were my way of checking how well I was understanding.

The Wizard was quick to respond. "Well said!
Centering takes you beyond your intellect to your being,
beyond what you have learned to be to what you actually
are. It takes you to what *is*. Centeredness is *how to be*."

It never failed. Whenever I seemed to mentally catch up
with the Wizard, he would take me one step beyond. It
was a constant game of catch-up. "The inner journey
takes me to what *is?* To my being? What then?"

"Your being, that which is authentically you, is open
and unbiased. It has no conscious limitations, no precon-
ceptions. As such, it provides you with the maximum
potential for creativity and change." The Wizard's manner was matter-of-fact.

Although this sounded good to me, I really didn't
understand it. My question was genuine: "How do I do
this?"

The Wizard chose a medical example to give scientific
authenticity to this elusive concept of *how to be*. "Dr.
Herbert Benson, President of the Mind/Body Institute in
Boston, has some insights on this. What began as a pro-

cess of reducing blood pressure has become a prerequisite for renewal. Benson found that the *relaxation response* or *meditation* opened the mind as well as the body to the forces of renewal. He discovered that the relaxation response evokes a greater harmony between the two halves of the brain, it makes it easier to process new information, and it enables us to see situations in new and creative ways. In short, the whole process of relaxation opens us up to change."

Assuming the mind and body are one, I knew the answer to the question I was about to ask, but I wanted to hear the Wizard's version. "Does physical relaxation give me a mental edge as well?"

"No doubt about it. Benson says the response gives anyone greater 'cognitive receptivity.' Another name for this is *beginner's mind,* an open and unbiased outlook. This enables you to approach any situation as a beginner, someone with everything to learn. In a relaxed state, you are most open to new approaches. This is the time to plant new ideas, the time when positive mental imagery and affirmations are more likely to take root and embed themselves in new patterns of behavior."

"It's like a fresh start?"

"For the moment, yes," assured the Wizard. "It is like setting the stopwatch back to zero so you can fully and accurately capture the moment without your prejudices and predispositions getting in the way. A relaxed state of being enables you to consider new initiatives, conflicting points of view, or creative approaches without your conscious mind rejecting them straight away. The unbounded nature of your being makes this possible. The intellect cannot give you a fair hearing. You have to get closer to your true center."

I didn't fully understand yet, but I knew with enough prompting that it would become clearer. "And this is why you call it centering?"

"Precisely. Not an easy thing for people to do, however. You might find it easier to understand if you think about what it means to be uncentered. You are *un*centered when you:

- have biases, predispositions, or fixed positions;
- feel insecure, guilty, depressed, anxious, or angry;
- have unrealistic expectations for your work associates, family, or self;
- prescribe "shoulds" for other people;
- try to change people exclusively for your own reasons; or
- allow yourself to be changed exclusively for others' reasons."

I shook my head. "You've just described me. I'm so off-center, it's a wonder I'm still upright!" With that, I suddenly jumped up on the trunk of a fallen Norway pine and extended my arms for balance. Carefully placing one foot in front of the other, I teetered uneasily for a few feet before losing my balance and jumping off. Turning to the Wizard and grinning with childlike glee, I asked, "Does this mean I'm psychologically unbalanced as well?"

The Wizard laughed heartily. He was obviously delighted. It was a sign I was less tense and feeling more comfortable with myself. "I feel better already!" I exclaimed.

"There is nothing like physical exertion," the Wizard said. "We are all uncentered to some degree. The problem with being uncentered, however, is that you see the world through your own depressed, anxious, or frustrated eyes. As such, you confuse your own personal needs with the demands of the situation and you get trapped in your own self-inflicted crises. This creates needless tension with non-problems, problems that would not be present if you took the time to center yourself."

"Needless tension with non-problems—that's the story of our times, isn't it, Wizard? If I could only bring my balanced self to each situation I face, I would eliminate most of my problems."

"This is why using your imagination is so important," stressed the Wizard, who was now drawing on our last encounter. "If you can envision what you would like to achieve, nearly every obstacle is a non-problem. In the context of a vision, any problem is simply a non-event. Having a vision channels your energy and enables you to transcend problems that would block others."

I then made a powerful observation. "What I really face is not the problems but *my attitude* toward those problems—and that is a choice that is up to me to make."

"Yes, and that is a choice no one can take from you— the right to choose your own attitude. Victor Frankl, author of *Man's Search for Meaning* and a holocaust survivor, calls this choice the last of the human freedoms. Nobody can put you down unless you allow it. If you feel put down, that is your choice. Other choices of how to feel, however, are available to you."

"It takes a very centered person to make those choices," I acknowledged with some futility in my voice.

"When you are uncentered, another person's untoward behavior can be a big problem for you," reasoned the Wizard. "To a centered person, however, the same problem may be dismissed as a mere eccentricity.

"The word *eccentric* means off-center. The behavior is 'off-center,' but it does not create a problem for the centered person. Eccentricity is part of the tapestry of life and at worst, it is an irritation. When you are balanced it takes a pretty solid hit to knock you off-balance. Whereas if you start off-balance, it does not take much to throw you even more off-center. Furthermore, when you start in-balance, you have a greater capacity to right yourself. The centered person is like a self-righting rescue ship. These ships are virtually incapable of capsizing."

I responded excitedly, "In England I've watched the ships from the Royal National Lifeboat Institute practice rescues. They're incredibly resiliant. When they roll over, they roll right back!"

"The resiliance of a centered person stems from the act of centering, and that is an energizing process. It is a restorative process that prepares you both to give and to receive energy. The power of centering lies in your ability to summon and to channel your energies for any occasion. I cannot make this point too strongly for business managers." The Wizard's tone became more serious.

"I am not advocating the monastic, introspective life for you, although that option is open to anyone. If you do not understand this process and if you fail to use it effectively, you risk being victimized by external events and circumstances. You become fodder, consumed by problems and crises. This is the trap many of us are in. I mentioned that earlier when we talked about urgent versus important matters."

"I'm glad you tied it back to that. It's all connected, isn't it? I really have to ask myself, Am I managing my business, or is my business managing me?"

"Yes, and without parents centering themselves, our families could turn from safe havens of support to scenes of abusive behavior, addiction, and despair. Just as athletes prepare by centering themselves, you should also center yourself for a meeting, a family outing, a confrontation, a negotiation, or whatever. Centering readies you to receive energy by opening yourself to your own creative source and to the energy of others. It also readies you to give by enhancing the quality of energy that emanates from you. This mutual exchange of energies is what managing business, family, and self is all about. To me, it is the placebo effect working its magic in management, just as it has always worked in medicine. This is the real secret of management, the untold story that will have to wait for another time. Waiting . . . ." the Wizard chuckled. "That is the way life is."

SUGGESTIONS

Now I had even more "Wizard homework." Add these relaxation and centering ideas to your positive affirmations and mental imagery practice:

* AS YOU MOVE FROM ONE SITUATION TO ANOTHER, TAKE TIME TO PAUSE BETWEEN THEM, EVEN IF JUST FOR A MOMENT. THIS MAY BE DONE AT THE DINNER TABLE, AT YOUR DESK BETWEEN MEETINGS, OR EVEN IN A MEETING. SIT COMFORTABLY, NOTHING CROSSED, WITH HANDS IN YOUR LAP OR ON YOUR THIGHS. TAKE SEVERAL DEEP BREATHS, BREATHING THROUGH YOUR NOSE. BRIEFLY, HOLD THE BREATHS, THEN EXHALE THROUGH THE NOSE. CLEAR YOUR MIND OF ALL THE EVENTS THAT PRECEDED THIS BREATHING. BE CONSCIOUS OF ANY MUSCLE TENSION. RELAX ANY TENSE MUSCLES. YOU WILL BEGIN TO FEEL YOUR BODY METABOLISM SLOWING DOWN.

 WITH PRACTICE, YOU CAN RELAX IN JUST A FEW MOMENTS. AT THE APPRO-PRIATE TIME, YOU MAY BEGIN TO THINK ABOUT THE NEXT BUSINESS MEETING OR FAMILY EVENT. BEFORE YOU BEGIN, VISUALIZE THE OUTCOME AS YOU WOULD LIKE IT TO BE. SEE IT WORKING OUT AS YOU WANT IT TO. WHEN YOU ARE READY, BEGIN TO TAKE ACTION TO ACHIEVE THE DESIRED OUTCOME.

* IN *YOUR MAXIMUM MIND,* DR. HERBERT BENSON RECOMMENDS THE FOL-LOWING "RELAXATION RESPONSE" AS CRUCIAL IN PRACTICALLY ANY SELF-HELP PROGRAM:

 STEP 1—PICK A FOCUS WORD OR SHORT PHRASE FIRMLY ROOTED IN YOUR PERSONAL BELIEF SYSTEM. FOR EXAMPLE, WORDS LIKE "LOVE" OR "ONE."

 STEP 2—SIT QUIETLY IN A COMFORTABLE POSITION.

 STEP 3—CLOSE YOUR EYES.

 STEP 4—RELAX YOUR MUSCLES.

 STEP 5—BREATHE SLOWLY AND NATURALLY, AND REPEAT YOUR FOCUS WORD TO YOURSELF AS YOU EXHALE.

 STEP 6—ASSUME A PASSIVE ATTITUDE. WHEN A DISTRACTING THOUGHT ENTERS YOUR MIND, GENTLY BRING YOUR ATTENTION BACK TO A FOCUS WORD. DON'T JUDGE, AND DON'T WORRY ABOUT HOW WELL YOU'RE DOING.

 STEP 7—CONTINUE FOR 10–20 MINUTES. PRACTICE THIS ENTIRE SEVEN-STEP PROCESS ONCE OR TWICE DAILY.

When you fulfill the belief that others have in you,
you discover the strength that lies within.

7

THE DOCTOR
WITHIN

What a difference words make! I kept reflecting on the Wizard's definition of management: getting people *done* through work. It's true that developing people, from work associates to children, is what management is all about. This new perception began to change the way I managed people. I could see clearly that changing my perception changes the way I do things. The mental images I had of my staff and family were changing, and so were my feelings and actions toward them.

I remembered what the Wizard had said earlier about healing and helping people become more whole. Getting people *done* through work is healing and making people whole. I realized, however, that I had much work to do on myself. My daily routine was so frenetic that I found I didn't always take the time to center myself between activities. But when I did, I noticed that things seemed to go a little smoother. Perhaps it was coincidental, but I felt a little more in control of things when I took a few moments to get myself together. Routinely centering myself was something I would have to work on, but I could definitely see merit in it.

In those quiet meditative moments, I did take some

time to practice positive mental imagery in areas where I had been previously negative. I focused on my health worries first, and slowly turned away from panic and despair. A new sense of optimism and a feeling of euphoria began to emerge along with my positive affirmations of life. I had always been told how difficult it was for people to change themselves, but I was finding this whole process to be a quietly transforming experience. I liked what was happening to me and I liked what was happening to the people I worked and lived with.

When we next met, the Wizard had just finished his usual lunch of fruits, whole grain foods, and fresh garden vegetables. "Wizard, I keep forgetting to ask you if you're a vegetarian."

"I am a vegetarian of sorts," he replied. "Most of us have far too much protein in our diets. Animal protein, our principal source, brings fat and cholesterol along with it. We have too much of those as well. Complex carbohydrates take less energy to metabolize—they burn more cleanly and I find I have more energy on a diet of complex carbohydrates. I get all the protein I need from other sources, but I am not opposed to fresh trout on occasion, especially if I have caught them."

"Each time we meet, I learn something new about you," I said with admiration. "I didn't know you were into nutrition."

"Actually, I am into energy, and nutrition plays a vital role in that regard."

"Speaking of energy, the last time we met you talked about the energy we exchange with others," I reminded, "and then you mentioned an 'untold story.'"

"You remembered!"

"How could I forget, Wizard, especially if it's as important as you say?"

"Sometimes I get a bit carried away with my statements, but there are some rather simple and profound truths about people, and I believe this is one of them. It is, perhaps, the real magic of management."

"I'm ready when you are."

The Wizard said, "When medical people refer to a *placebo,* do you know what they mean?"

"I believe so. That's the sugar pill, isn't it?"

"Yes, but it is much more than that."

"With you, it always is," I needled.

The two of us shared a laugh as the Wizard offered me a slice of homegrown honeydew melon.

"I guess good food is why I keep coming to see you," I joked. "But what else is a placebo?"

"It is any pill, potion, or procedure that has no direct effect on a patient's illness," said the Wizard, "but the patient *believes* it will work."

"So it's not the pill itself but the patient that makes the real difference."

"Precisely." The Wizard seemed pleased. "The great British physician, Sir William Osler, said it was more important to know what *person* has a disease than what *disease* a person has. The idea, my friend, is to treat people, not diseases."

"So it's a matter of where the doctor puts his energies, on the disease or on the patient?"

"Yes. The same mistake is made in education when we teach courses rather than people." The Wizard loved to make comparisons.

"You've identified a very subtle difference," I allowed.

"My use of language is subtle, but the difference is quite immense. Many scholars believe the history of medicine is the history of the placebo effect. What is important is not just the treatment, but the patient's belief that the treatment will work. If they see themselves recovering, then these innocuous little potions often work their wondrous ways."

"So what does all this placebo talk have to do with management?" I challenged.

"Plenty," insisted the Wizard. "You see, the belief can be as important as the treatment. A placebo is really an image of healing in the mind of the patient. The image transforms itself into healing through that three-step process you and I discussed some time ago."

"You mean the image-feeling-action cycle?"

"Yes."

"We talked then, as I recall, about using mental imagery to break old habit patterns, to see new possibilities, and to go 'beyond the walls.' Now you're saying a placebo is imagery, and it also has healing powers?"

The Wizard explained, "Mental imagery is one way you 'talk' to your body. The other way is through your emotions. Positive emotions and positive imagery stimulate the healing process. The science of PNI, psychoneuroimmunology, is breaking new ground in linking emotions to the immune system. In this context, imagination, or mental imagery, is the greatest healer. It is the magical nexus that holds the body and the mind together."

"What I have on my mind affects how I feel and what I do," I remembered.

"If you can psyche yourself into getting sick, you can also psyche yourself into getting well and staying well," continued the Wizard. "We know that negative emotions such as depression and anxiety weaken the immune system, while positive emotions such as love and forgiveness strengthen it. If you see yourself getting better with positive expectations, then you are setting the stage for the body to heal itself. An estimated 85% of all people seeking medical help suffer from self-limiting disorders well within their capabilities to heal themselves."

"85%?" I reacted with surprise.

"Yes, the late Franz Inglefinger, editor of the *New England Journal of Medicine,* wrote that 85% of human illnesses are within reach of the body's own healing system. Remember, doctors do not heal. They are only channels. In effect, a doctor simply gives you permission to heal yourself. Putting it more accurately, you give yourself permission. All healing is self-healing in this regard. The best medical help is only as good as the images our mind will allow."

"Once again, it's up to us," I said. "So my negative images can negate positive medical intervention . . . ."

"The late Norman Cousins concluded ten years of mind-body research by saying, 'Patients tend to move along the path of their expectations, whether on the upside or on the downside,' " recounted the Wizard. "Often, the patient's mindset disallows medical help."

"Are you saying that the placebo is a patient's positive expectation?"

"Yes, all of the helping professions are alike in that they encourage patients to take charge of their lives and do something positive for themselves," said the Wizard. "When asked what a doctor could do, one well-known surgeon suggested two things: first, the doctor could give patients control over their own treatment; and second, the doctor could offer hope."

I'm sure I looked a little stunned. "That's amazing, coming from a surgeon. It sounds more like good management advice—turn the job over to your staff and demonstrate your confidence in them to do it."

"You just made the management connection you asked about earlier, and you are right. That *is* good advice. If you are programmed with habitually self-defeating images of yourself, the treatment simply will not work. When you replace negative images with positive ones, you redirect your energies toward healing. The job of the doctor is to open the patient to the process of healing," avowed the Wizard.

"The placebo is obviously a lot more than I thought it was," I confessed.

"The placebo comes in three stages," the Wizard explained. "The first and most elementary stage is the pill itself. Most people need something tangible to equate with getting well. Ingesting a pill, getting a shot, or taking medicine in some other form does this. It tells you that something good physically will come of this. A prescription from a doctor you trust is tangible assurance of getting well."

"It makes sense that if my symptoms are tangible, I ought to deal with them tangibly—with a pill," I agreed.

"That is the easiest connection for most people to make. The second placebo stage involves only the relationship with the doctor. At this stage, all you need is reassurance. The effect hinges on the confidence you have in the doctor and in your conviction that the doctor takes you seriously. Here, the doctor is the placebo. More specifically, the placebo is the quality of the relationship between you and the doctor. Your belief that the doctor cares makes you receptive to suggestion. Francis Peabody said, 'The secret of the care of the patient is in caring for the patient.'"

"Here all we need is the doctor's word?"

"Or the doctor's touch. When a mother kisses her child's skinned knee, she is performing a healing act. She is the placebo."

I smiled knowingly. "Well, I'm beginning to see the whole connection."

"There is more," said the Wizard.

I shrugged, feigning resignation. "I know, I know. There is always more."

"The third and highest placebo stage takes place within

you," declared the Wizard. "At this level, my friend, you do not need tangible effects or even reassurance. Instead of needing externals, your intuitive sense tells you what is best. Norman Cousins, in his classic book *Anatomy of an Illness,* recalls Dr. Albert Schweitzer telling him one of medicine's secrets: 'Each patient carries his own doctor inside him. They come to us not knowing the truth. We are at our best when we give the doctor who resides within each patient a chance to go to work.' At this stage, the placebo is the 'doctor within.' "

"That is the first thing you told me when we met," I recollected. "The answers you seek lie within you."

"I am gratified that you remember," said the Wizard. "All three placebo stages have one thing in common—a *belief* in recovery. All have the expectation, the hope, and the will to recover. Belief is much more powerful than any external technique."

"Belief is more powerful than technique," I repeated. "That statement is powerful."

"It is powerful because you believe it. I believe the placebo effect works in all the healing professions. The doctor, the therapist, the coach, the teacher, the business manager, the parent—all have placebo power. The vast majority of people are at the first placebo stage. At this stage, you need *things* to help you feel okay about yourself. You need to validate your worth externally because you are not sure of yourself internally. Status symbols are the big consideration here. These are the 'sugar pills' of management. You recall in *The Wizard of Oz,* the Cowardly Lion received a medal for bravery from Oz. He wanted courage, and this was tangible evidence.

"Significantly fewer people operate at the second placebo stage. Here you only need the *reassurance* of the manager, the healing touch. This reinforcing or reaffirming act is a vital and continuous part of the management process.

At stage two, the manager is the placebo.

"Very few people have reached the point where they are able to function fully and effectively at the third placebo stage. This level requires faith, a strong sense of personal worth, and a confidence that comes from the inner journey. At this stage, you do not need external reassurance in the form of things and people. You know intuitively what you need to do."

"Why the need for stage three? Why not just give people management 'pills' at stage one and be done with it?" I quizzed the Wizard. "Surely you aren't saying we should forsake the tangibles like pay and perks and toys for some hoped-for internal satisfaction."

"Far from it," argued the Wizard. "Everyone wants to embrace life fully. You and your staff and family need the tangibles and the reassurances from the people you admire and respect. The idea, if you recall, is to turn the treatment over to the patient. If you do not move beyond the first two placebo stages, you will forever be dependent upon them. It is only by reaching stage three that you can live freely at the other two. Then you do not have to have them. If you do not have to have something, you are free to choose what is best for you. You are less likely to be victimized by those who exploit and manipulate these rewards for their own purposes. You are not dependent on things or on others. The 'doctor within' prescribes what is best for you."

"Now I see what you mean. The pill is only a short-term fix. Presumably, the only way I can erase my dependency is to develop my inner resources—what you call the 'doctor within.'"

"Precisely! You want to get beyond the debilitating constraints of dependency," urged the Wizard. "Our age of specialization is an age of fragmentation. You have learned helplessness, an acquired dependence on specialists. Medicine is just one of those specialties. You need to re-establish control over your own life. This is what the 'doctor within' can do for you. You need doctors and other specialists, but the locus of control in your life must remain with *you*. You cannot abdicate that responsibility. Passively taking placebo pills does not prepare you to accept that responsibility."

"That's a lesson we need to learn in business," I injected. "And in the home."

"You are so right. Developing your inner resources gives you the strength to avoid becoming a victim of power games. If you need something—like keeping your job or getting respect—that others control, they have power over you and they could take advantage of you."

"That's very unsettling . . . ."

"Yes," said the Wizard, "and sadly, control is the basis of much organizational insecurity in the business world, not to mention power struggles between parents and children in the family. Management by fear has always been with us. It is premised on making you feel you have no choice but to comply. However, if you value what others have or do for you but you do not have to have it or do it, then you have options. This enables you to work with others more creatively. You can opt out of all those unproductive power games by not being a victim."

The Wizard excused himself from the room for a moment. When he returned, he offered me a glass of his homemade hand-pressed apple cider. I tasted the cider—it was delicious—and then held the glass out in front of me to eye the turbid liquid.

"Mm-m-m-m! That's so much better than the clear cider." Reflecting on the Wizard's comment about not being a victim, I mused, "We always come back to our inner selves, don't we?"

"The answers you seek . . ." the Wizard began.

". . . lie within you," I finished. "It makes more sense to me now than the first time I heard it. But I have a question for you: If very few of us function at this inner stage three, what are my chances for developing the 'doctor within'?"

"There is always hope," said the Wizard with a look of expectancy. "Hope itself is a powerful placebo. Alone, it has healing powers that make you receptive to change."

"But what can I specifically do as a manager of my business, my home . . . and myself?"

"Exercise placebo power at all three stages," declared the Wizard. "Cover the needs at stage one with the necessary tangibles, the material things. Be a living placebo at stage two with your 'touch.' And get people *done* through work at stage three. Offer your family members and your workforce the opportunity to develop themselves by making a difference in your home and in your company. This involves all that we have talked about and more—energizing possibilities, balancing the urgent and the important, learning the power of concentration to unify inner calm and outer action, releasing your energies, and opening yourself to the energies of others. It is a lifetime job. But what an exciting one it is! Everything your family and staff do in the home and on the job is an investment in themselves. They are empowered within the family or self-employed with the company, and that is the best of both worlds."

"Wizard, I think I've got it, but could you sum this up just one more time?" It was all so new to me!

"At stage one, you need *things* to tell you that you are okay. This is blatantly apparent in America, where people need monogrammed clothing to convince themselves and others that they belong. At stage two, you need *people* whom you respect to reassure you that you are okay. At stage three, you have weaned yourself away from being dependent upon externals. Here, *you know intuitively* that you and others have worth and are okay. The 'doctor within' has told you so. Your job as a manager is to use your placebo power to help others free themselves by getting beyond the dependency of the first two stages. Placebo power gives you a three-stage process for developing the 'doctor within.' It is the real magic of management, indeed, of life itself," concluded the Wizard.

"I know I have a long way to go, yet if you hadn't believed in me, I would never have come this far. You've helped me at a very stressful time in my life. I owe you a lot, Wizard."

"You owe me nothing, but you owe your staff and your family members something. Do for them as you say I have done for you," urged the Wizard. "It all begins with belief in a person's potential. When you believe in the potential of others, you energize that potential. You potentiate people, empowering them to release their energies and go 'beyond the walls.' This is placebo power, the enduring message in *The Wizard of Oz*. When you fulfill the belief that others have in you, you will surely discover the strength that lies within. That strength is the 'doctor within,' and that is *how to be.*"

"Thank you. I appreciate hearing how I can grow and help others, too."

"You are most welcome. Building your practice for the 'doctor within' demands that you employ powers of the mind vastly superior to your rational powers. I refer to the irrational power of intuition. But now my 'doctor within' tells me that is a story for another time. That is the way life is."

SUGGESTIONS

The Wizard had me ask myself and others the following questions:

* STAGE ONE—WHAT ARE SOME TANGIBLE PLACEBOS I NEED TO CONFIRM MY OKAY-NESS?

* STAGE TWO—WHO ARE SOME OF THE PEOPLE I DEPEND UPON TO REASSURE ME OF MY OKAY-NESS?

* STAGE THREE—WHAT DO I NEED FROM MYSELF AND FROM OTHERS TO DEVELOP MY "DOCTOR WITHIN"?

Ask the following questions concerning your key people at work (or substitute each of your family members here):

* STAGE ONE—WHAT TANGIBLE PLACEBOS CAN I ADMINISTER TO THEM TO CONFIRM THEIR OKAY-NESS?

* STAGE TWO—WHAT INTANGIBLE PLACEBOS CAN I PERSONALLY OFFER TO REASSURE THEM OF THEIR OKAY-NESS?

* STAGE THREE—WHAT ARE SOME THINGS I CAN DO TO HELP THEM DEVELOP THEIR "DOCTOR WITHIN"?

Give each person the first three questions you asked yourself.

Have them reflect upon them for a day or so while you ask yourself the second set of three questions.

Compare your "findings" with theirs.

Use the questions and responses as the basis for a personal development discussion.

Individually, have that discussion with each person.

The curse of consciousness is to see the world in bits and pieces.

8

THE CURSE OF CONSCIOUSNESS

I was quite moved by my latest visit with the Wizard. First, I decided to take more time to reflect on the power of belief and my "doctor within." I felt a greater sense of aliveness as I accepted the challenge of moving my staff and my family from their near total dependency on material, tangible things to the inner confidence that I was beginning to experience. I knew if I was to be the healer in all of my interactions with them, in my "manager" role, I must be a whole person. If doctors practice medicine, I must practice management. It was, of course, crucial to my own health and well-being that I heal myself in the process.

Practicing implies developing one's skills. Even the most accomplished physicians, musicians, and athletes continue to practice. Practice makes them more complete, more whole. There were moments when I actually felt like *I* was the Wizard because of the connections I was making. These were heady times. My mind was swimming as I thought about all the how-to-be ideas from my meeting with the Wizard. I was excited about the possibilities opening in my life. What the Wizard said about possibilities was really true: They do excite!

I could feel a difference in myself now, compared to the frustration and fatigue I felt a few months ago when I sought out the Wizard. Recalling the Wizard's statement that the answers lay within me, I now realized they were beginning to emerge as the "doctor within."

One dark cloud loomed on my horizon. For some time I had a sore on the back of my left hand that resisted healing. As a young person I spent a lot of time in the sun and, being fair-skinned, I had the potential for developing skin cancer in later years. The Wizard had made me more aware of my overall health. It was time I did something about this.

Several weeks passed before we met again. When we did, it was as if no time had gone by. The Wizard said that was the mark of a good relationship. A light rain was falling as the two of us moved into his house. The Wizard built a fire in the study while I told him how much better I was feeling and the deep stirring of excitement and hope I felt inside.

"It sounds as if the 'doctor within' is making rounds," the Wizard noted, his face alive with satisfaction. "I am so pleased you are having this renaissance of feelings, for this is what will stir you to take positive action. And action is what life is all about."

"Last time, you said that in order to build my practice for the 'doctor within,' I needed to employ intuition—an irrational power greater than reason." I fixed my eyes on the Wizard wondering what he really meant. "That struck me as a rather curious statement."

"It *is* curious, isn't it?" admitted the Wizard. "Let me tell you a story from 1982 about the first enemy engagement of the Falklands War, the battle of Goose Green. Major Christopher Keeble of the elite 2nd Battalion, the Parachute Regiment, assumed leadership when his commanding officer was killed in a gallant assault on an

Argentine machine gun position. From the beginning, the British battalion had been outnumbered three to one. The situation deteriorated as the day wore on. At dusk, Major Keeble felt all options except retreat seemed futile. The men in his battalion pressed Major Keeble for a decision. Unwilling to retreat and not knowing what else to do, he walked a few steps away from his men. In a small ravine, alone with his thoughts, he said a short prayer: 'My Father, I abandon myself to you. Do with me as you will. I am ready for anything. I accept everything provided your will is fulfilled in me. I ask for nothing more.'

"As Major Keeble tells the story, he was immediately suffused with a feeling of peacefulness and hope and, for the first time since the battalion had landed, he was not aware of the biting cold. In those few quiet moments, the germ of an amazing idea came to him. Why not a peaceful solution? Here were two Christian forces killing each other. It was madness. His idea, incongruous as it seemed to be, was to offer the enemy commander a surrender with honor! His message would be love, not bloodshed.

"When he returned to his men and presented his idea, they thought he was mad, but he persisted. Working with his signalman, Major Keeble released two prisoners with a message requesting to meet the enemy commander. When they met, the enemy officers appeared in spotless dress uniforms, while he and his officers 'reeked of violence and death' in full combat gear. Major Keeble, with steely-eyed will, told the commander that his 2nd Battalion had come 10,000 miles and were not about to stop 100 yards short of their goal. The enemy was given the option of a surrender with honors in a full dress parade, or be overwhelmed. The Argentine commander *accepted* the offer, and the British regiment celebrated its first victory of the war."

"Astonishing! But why would the Argentinians surrender when they were winning?" I wondered.

"Perhaps they did not know they were winning; but that is not the point," said the Wizard. "Let us not lose sight of the purpose of the story. Without open space, that quiet meditative moment, the germ of a peaceful solution would not have flowered. Major Keeble could not even have perceived it. The solution was not the result of rational thought. It was intuitive or 'irrational.' We cannot summon intuition as we can summon reason. To employ the power of intuition, we can only prepare ourselves to receive it."

"You've certainly piqued my interest."

"I fear I must get a bit theoretical again. Can a person of action like you stand another metaphysical discourse?" the Wizard asked, in a mock-professorial manner.

"I've survived your other talks without serious side effects," I replied. With my arms outstretched and my eyes cast downward, I pretended to scan my body for negative side effects. "Try me once more."

The Wizard rose from his chair to attend to the fire. He placed three logs pyramid-style on top of the kindling which, by now, was burning well. Then he settled back into his chair, winked at me, and began to speak.

"Nature has no walls. The natural world you live in is an unbroken whole, a seamless panorama. But because the whole is too vast for the conscious mind to grasp, you are blessed with five senses and an analytical mind to fathom this whole. With these faculties, you can literally break the natural world into bite-size pieces to make sense of it.

"You see it, touch it, hear it, taste it, smell it, and analyze it in detail to know more about it. This breakdown process is *differentiation*. Your conscious mind looks for differences. It discriminates one thing from another by separation—different appearances, sounds, etc. But this blessing is also a curse. The *curse of consciousness* is to see the world in its separateness, to constantly perceive it in bits and pieces."

"Curse of consciousness?"

"Consciousness separates," said the Wizard. "Therefore, in order to integrate the pieces of the world into a whole, you must get beyond the conscious mind, beyond the limitation of your senses. That is what intuition does for all people.

"Over the millennia, the human body has developed a certain wisdom in surviving. It immunizes itself against foreign substances and copes with stress, for example. This wisdom of the body is programmed into your genetic inheritance. In a like manner, your mind has a wisdom of its own in the unconscious. Call it the collective unconscious, if you will. This wisdom, too, is part of your genetic endowment. In this context, you 'know' all you need to know from the beginning. This is the wisdom of the ages. The key question is, how can you access it?

"Intuition alone has access to the unconscious mind, that limitless unknown that lies beyond your consciousness. It has the power of integration, the capacity to synthesize the fragments of the conscious mind with glimpses of insight into the whole of life. Where the rational conscious mind separates the whole, the 'irrational' unconscious mind integrates it. This is the mind's true healing power, my friend."

"How can I access all that intuitive healing power?" I asked. "It would . . . come in handy."

"Everything begins with awareness, yet to be aware of anything, you must first bring it to your consciousness. Do you know who controls your conscious mind?" The Wizard liked to answer questions with questions.

"My boss!" I said laughingly. Then in a quick reversal of mood, I became serious again. "No. Who?"

"You said that lightly, I know," observed the Wizard, "but the power to choose your own state of mind is the last of the human freedoms. It is frightening how readily many of us relinquish this right on a regular basis."

"I know all too well," I said, sounding a bit victimized. "That's why I have to develop my 'doctor within.' It sounds as if intuition and the 'doctor within' have a lot in common. But, I apologize—you were about to tell me who controls my conscious mind . . . ."

"I am glad you distracted me for a bit—I love distractions. They are often more productive than the subject that gives rise to them. But here is the answer to your question: The CEO of your conscious mind is the *ego*. For you to be aware of anything, it must first pass through your consciousness, and that is under the tight supervision of the ego. Intuition does not stand a chance—it simply does not function—as long as the ego is in charge."

"Now that's power!" I said with a knowing smile.

"You bet it is, and do not think for a moment that the ego hesitates to use the power," said the Wizard, pointing his finger in a commanding manner. "I believe this is management's biggest problem. This is also a parent's greatest downfall."

"Ego is the biggest problem?"

"Yes," declared the Wizard, "Ego has created problems throughout history. Joseph Campbell taught us that dragons and other ogres are common to all cultures. The hero must slay the dragon, symbolic of the ego, to continue the personal journey. The mythic passage symbolizes what we call the inner journey.

"Campbell wrote, 'It has always been the prime function of mythology and rite to supply the symbols that carry the human spirit forward.' Myths teach us symbolically how to take the human spirit forward with the inner journey. Scientific materialism has de-mythologized our culture and obliterated the historic benchmarks for the inner journey. As a result, the growth of the human spirit has been stunted.

"In business and in the home, our excessive need for control stunts the spirit. The spirit needs release, not control. Overly authoritative parents stifle the development of a child's creative powers. This process of suppression continues when controlling supervisors pick up where parents left off. This is the work of the ego, which has a need to control its turf. Because it cannot control the unconscious which is the source of intuition, it ignores it or demeans it. In doing so, the ego denies itself access to its vast integrative powers.

"The ego has another more immediate problem. Unable to see beyond the fragments of life, the ego assumes that the pieces are the whole. When another person's ego sees different bits, the two argue endlessly over bits and pieces. Do you recall that wonderful childhood fable about the blind men and the elephant?"

The Wizard reached up and pulled a colorful volume of children's fables from his bookshelf. Smiling, he turned to me and said, "This should be a part of everyone's library. Six blind men, each with a grasp on a different part of the elephant, made a comparison—tusk like a spear, tail like a rope, trunk like a snake, ear like a fan, side like a wall, and knee like a tree."

With that, he riffled through the pages, adjusted his glasses, and read the conclusion to *The Blind Men and the Elephant* by John Geoffrey Saxe:

> *And so these men of Indostan*
> *Disputed loud and long,*
> *Each in his own opinion*
> *Exceeding stiff and strong,*

Though each was partly in the right
And all were in the wrong.

As oft in theologic wars
The disputants, I ween,
Rail on in utter ignorance
Of what each other mean,
And prate about an elephant
Not one of them has seen.

"Such wisdom, and written over 100 years ago!" exclaimed the Wizard. "All of us are guilty of 'prating' about the elephant of life that no one has 'seen.' We are experts on the tusk and the tail, but we know almost nothing of the whole. We know almost nothing of *how to be* in life."

"How do we see the whole?" I asked.

The Wizard drew an imaginary sword from his side, saying, "Suppress the ego." Then he thrust the sword home with a playful shout of, "Slay the dragon!" Sheathing his make-believe weapon, he continued. "You have to open yourself to the reality that your perception is but a small part, only a piece of the whole, and acknowledge that others can contribute more pieces with their perceptions. Rather than fighting over who is right, you can accept that each of us is only partly in the right, but together we can grasp more of the whole. That makes the business manager more respectful of other co-workers and parents more receptive to their children."

Once again I probed. "And *how* do we do this?"

"I think there are two preconditions, my friend," answered the Wizard. "One is to accept full responsibility for yourself. This requires confidence in your own intuition, the placebo power of the 'doctor within.' A great spokesman for this confident spirit is Vaclav Havel, the dissident playwright who became the first president of the new Czech Republic."

Searching through a well-thumbed reading pile, the Wizard pulled out a yellowing newspaper. Moving his finger quickly down the columns, he briefly stopped and smiled, obviously enjoying a passage. At last he found the part he was looking for.

"Speaking to a joint session of the U. S. Congress, Havel said, 'We are still incapable of understanding that the only genuine backbone of all our actions, if they are to be moral, is responsibility—responsibility to something higher than my family, my country, my company, my success. If I subordinate my political behavior to this imperative, mediated to me by my conscience, I can't go far wrong.' Your *conscience,* what you know to be true, will keep your ego in check. Havel has enormous integrity because, at great personal sacrifice, he never accepted communist rule."

"He backed his words with deeds," I agreed. "You said there were *two* preconditions . . . ."

"Yes, of course. Thank you. The other precondition is open space. Everyone needs time to reflect upon the moral responsibility Havel talks about. When you urge people to accept the baton of responsibility, they need time and space to integrate what it really means. This is creative, unstructured time. The concept has to travel from the head to the heart, for the heart is the only place where we truly *know.* It will tell us *how to be.* So long as the concept of self-responsibility is only an idea in our head, it is fragile and easily replaced by a better idea. The heart is the center of the self, the goal of our inner journey, the core of our being. When the heart knows, commitment follows."

"That's heavy."

"It is also very relevant," claimed the Wizard. "You are

talking about knowing what's right and doing it. Your conscience knows right from wrong. To Havel, it is a choice 'to live within the truth.' In his essay, 'The Power of the Powerless,' he writes about the 'singular, explosive, incalculable power' of this hidden sphere of truth which grows from within, with a life lived openly in the truth."

I barely held on to a thin thread of understanding, but I continued to ask my trademark practical questions. "And how do I know 'the truth'?"

"You have to sort it out for yourself," said the Wizard. "That is Havel's message, and that is what taking responsibility is all about. To be responsible requires space for personal reflection."

The Wizard put another log on the fire and then momentarily excused himself. He returned with a handful of seed corn. Laying it on the table in front of me, he said, "I will plant these different strains of seed corn in the spring. In a memorable speech that led to the first nuclear test ban, President Kennedy said, 'If we cannot end now our differences, at least we can help make the world safe for diversity.' With differences comes diversity, and diversity is as vital to the health of society as it is to agriculture. In nature, diversity insures survival. The different genetic strains of this corn will guarantee its survival. So it is with ideas. In the 1980s and early 1990s, the total collapse of communism all across Eastern Europe was due to the absence of political diversity. The challenge today is to manage diversity by allowing the free expression of differences. In effect, this means de-managing or exercising less control. This is a threat to ego, the great turf protector. Managers, parents—everyone—need to learn to let go."

"Let go of what?"

"Ego. Control. Fear. Inhibitions. Stress. Habits. Old ways of doing things. This need to let go is a curious paradox. In letting go, you actually gain control of a different kind. You acquire the energies and commitments of those whom you *allow* to participate. The key is in allowing, not in controlling, however. Orchestrating this participative diversity is one of the biggest challenges for leadership today, and knowing when to let go is critical. The latter requires *humility.*"

"Humility?"

"Yes," said the Wizard. "If you have all the answers as a business manager or as a parent, you do not need others except to carry out your wishes...but that day is gone. Metaphorically speaking, you cannot add water to a full glass. Humility is emptying your 'glass' for the moment, so that you may be open to anything."

"So humility is openness?"

"That is a good part of it, my friend," said the Wizard. "We all think we are open, but few of us really are. Humility is the 'beginner's mind.' If you know it all, you cannot learn anything new. That is the problem with ego and, I am afraid, with experts. It is impossible to become a true expert if you already think you are. Certainty gets in your way. Ashley Montagu says, 'Only absolute fools are absolutely certain.'

"Remember, the images you have inside you overpower the images that come from the outside. So you have to neutralize those internal mindsets in order to get an unbiased perception. That is why we need a heavy dose of humility. This may sound a bit old-fashioned, but humility is truly a timeless quality. Being humble is *how to be.* That is the way life is."

SUGGESTIONS

As I faced coping with health concerns and reorienting my life, the Wizard suggested the following process. I know it will help you, too:

* IF YOU HAVE AN IMPORTANT DECISION TO MAKE OR A BIG PROBLEM TO SOLVE, IMMERSE YOURSELF IN THE SITUATION. CONCENTRATE TOTALLY AND SOAK UP ALL THE INFORMATION YOU CAN.

* AFTER A PERIOD OF INTENSE EFFORT, IF THE ANSWERS ARE NOT FORTHCOMING, DON'T FORCE THEM. THROUGH INTENSE CONCENTRATION, YOU HAVE TOLD YOUR UNCONSCIOUS MIND THAT THIS IS IMPORTANT.

* NOW TAKE TIME TO "SLEEP ON IT." IF SLEEP IS NOT APPROPRIATE, WALK AWAY FROM IT AND LET YOUR UNCONSCIOUS MIND WORK ITS WONDROUS WAYS WHILE YOU PURSUE SOMETHING TRIVIAL OR LEISURELY. THIS IS THE CRITICAL INCUBATION STAGE OF CREATIVITY.

* ANSWERS MANIFEST THEMSELVES OFTEN IN STRANGE WAYS, SO BE OPEN TO ALL SIGNS AND SIGNALS. INSIGHT USUALLY COMES IN FLASHES. IT CANNOT BE COERCED, NOR CONTROLLED. IT CAN ONLY BE ALLOWED TO HAPPEN. THIS IS OFTEN IN A RELAXED MOMENT WHEN WE LEAST EXPECT IT.

* IF NOTHING HAPPENS, TAKE ANOTHER RUN AT THE DECISION OR PROBLEM WHEN YOU ARE FRESH, AND THEN REPEAT THE PROCESS. INSIGHTS *WILL* COME. YOUR TASK IS SIMPLY TO BE SUFFICIENTLY RELAXED AND AWARE TO NOTICE THESE ANSWERS FROM WITHIN.

9

THE DRAGON
SLAYER

It was a difficult time for me in the weeks that followed. My fears about skin cancer were confirmed. The doctor called and said the biopsies showed malignancy. Immediately I had the lesion surgically removed. This form of skin carcinoma is life-threatening only if it has spread. At the time, I didn't know if it had. It was impossible tuning out these health concerns, my family problems, and my business crises—intuition was eluding me. I understood what the Wizard said about responsibility, but open space was very elusive. Presumably, intuition comes when I give myself some space, like the account of Major Keeble in the Falklands. Was this the same as the "doctor within"?

It took many days for me to finally settle down. Then I prayed for my own healing and the healing of those around me. Perhaps that did some good, for I began to feel calmer. I still had lots of questions, but for the first time I was mentally able to reconstruct our last session so I could anticipate the next level of healing the Wizard would introduce me to.

I began talking to myself: "Apparently my conscious mind can't deal with the vast whole of nature. With its analytical reasoning powers, my mind breaks the natural world down into separate components. As a result, I learn more and more about less and less. In order to make sense out of this, I need to integrate these bits back into the larger context of life. The Hindu fable illustrated that the tusk of an elephant has meaning only in the context of the whole animal. Intuition can provide me with access to the "elephant of life" by giving me fleeting glimpses of the whole. This is the gestalt, the illumination stage in the creative process. It is that moment when everything comes together in one flash of insight."

I continued talking to myself: "Nothing comes to my consciousness except through the ego. In order for my intuition to work, I have to neutralize the ego. Apparently that's the role of humility."

I was relieved that I could recall the essence of what I thought the Wizard had said. But more important, for the first time I was able to anticipate what I thought the Wizard was going to say next. When I heard him mention the word humility, I didn't have a beginner's mind. I had always passed humility off lightly like Churchill did when he spoke derisively of a Labor prime minister as having "much to be humble about."

I realized that I had been biased against humility. My conscious mind had not given humility a fair hearing. And I definitely was not centered. Consciously, I now allowed my beginner's mind to explore other interpretations of humility and its *how-to-be* importance. In the past I would have taken my bias to the Wizard, laid it out for him, then waited to be convinced otherwise—which only the Wizard could do. It was reassuring to know how I had caught myself this time, without being reminded. And then it struck me—the "doctor within" was at work! A quiet sense of satisfaction came over me. I closed my eyes and savored the moment.

When we next met, the Wizard had some photos spread on the table before him. He invited me to join him at the table. "Have you been on a trip?" I inquired.

"It was more like a trek," replied the Wizard. "For most of us, life is no longer an adventure. It has become a habit—routine and predictable, and not very exciting. I need to trek periodically to step outside my regimen and renew my sense of aliveness."

"And that does it?" I asked with eyebrows raised.

"Like nothing else. A wilderness trek allows me to engage in and reflect upon challenging experiences. That is what life is all about—*action* and *reflection*. Most business managers and parents are long on action and short on reflection, yet it is the reflective side of life that gives meaning and purpose to the action. A trek enables you to test yourself and learn from the experience with undiluted, immediate, unforgiving feedback. You cannot 'con' nature. Nature is not responsive to games and has no time for politics, nor does it respond to autocratic demands. In short, the challenge of nature gets you out of your comfort zone and helps you break through your self-imposed limitations."

"It does all that?" I asked incredulously.

"And more," said the Wizard. "There is nothing like nature to sort out your priorities. Life is very elemental, but everyone complicates it so. The natural world puts life back into perspective. You need nature to activate your sense of wonder and to evoke your latent humility."

"Humility," I repeated. "That's where we left off last time. Let me tell you, it really threw me for a while. Humility sounded so wimpish, but I promised myself I would be open to new meanings."

"That is wise, for you will come to appreciate humility's awesome power," the Wizard asserted, peering over the top of his glasses.

"The awesome power of humility?"

"Absolutely. Humility is the key to breaking the ego barrier. It is the dragon slayer. Like the blind men from Indostan, if you have blind convictions that you are always right, you are not open to others. Your fixed opinions are mindsets that prevent choice and lock you into only one interpretation. There can be no creativity, no co-mingling of ideas and energies among people when you are not open. Without it, you will miss countless *how-to-be* opportunities on the job and at home. Humility is a centering act."

"But how do I practice humility?" I asked.

"Commune with nature. Observe a child at play. Contemplate a light year. Give . . ."

"A light year?" I interrupted.

"Yes. Have you ever really paused to think about a light year? It is the distance light travels in one year. This is the standard measurement for outer space, the cosmic equivalent to our earth-bound mile. Light travels at l86,000 miles per second. One light year is 5.88 trillion miles. That is 5.88 thousand, thousand, thousand, thousand miles! When I realize that the nearest star is 4.3 light years away, or 25 trillion miles, I feel a deep sense of humility. This grows when I realize the Hubble space telescope can see stars 14 billion light years away. How many miles is 5.88 trillion times 14 billion?"

"It puts things into perspective . . . ."

"In working with people," the Wizard shifted to his practical mode, "I recommend two preconditions for humility: First, you simply set aside your fixed opinions so that they do not block the exchange of ideas and energies; and second, you accept the other person unconditionally as having worth and being capable of contributing. This is an operational definition of humility."

"Simply said is not simply done," I asserted, recalling

the Wizard's repeated claim that simple is not easy.

"I have said that ego pride is a manager's biggest problem," stated the Wizard, "whether you are managing a business, a family, or yourself. Historically, ego pride has been labeled the cardinal *sin*. If so, then humility is the cardinal *virtue.*"

"You're sounding rather pious," I joked.

"I am only being practical, my friend. How else can you or anyone else get the blinders off and see the whole elephant? You have such an adversary tradition in the West that you fail to see how opposites complement each other. You think of light and darkness only as opposites, but if you look at the whole, they complement each other. In the absence of darkness, light has no meaning. It is death that makes life precious. Without evil, what would be the meaning of goodness? If we accept pride, we must also have humility."

I glanced, distracted, at those darker patches of brown on the backs of my hands and wondered if they too were precancerous. They looked like benign "liver spots," so common with aging skin, but now I had reason to doubt—and doubt is corrosive to healing.

"Are you saying that when I have differences with my doctor, my children or my business partner, that I should not look at the conflicting points of view?"

The Wizard turned to the photos on the table and selected a variety of shots—pictures of wild flowers, colorful lichen, rock faces, moss and incense cedar bark, conifer seedlings, mountain streams and water ouzels, sapsuckers and Coulter pinecones, and gray squirrels and Stellar jays. After I had looked at each picture, the Wizard handed me a broad panorama shot of the whole wilderness area, taken with a wide-angle lens.

"In nature, everything is different, yet each piece fits into the larger scheme of things. When you change just one element in an ecosystem, all the other elements are affected. As such, the differences between these diverse elements can only be understood in the context of the whole. When you look at the big picture, you will learn to value differences. Two of your business colleagues may argue from different positions, but in the larger context, they both want what is best for your company. Your family is made up of very different individuals, but each person counts and everyone must have their needs met so your whole family can thrive. This shared perception gives a new slant to everyone's differences."

"It all sounds good," I agreed, "but how can I embrace the whole when I have genuine differences with others?"

"Accept the differences, but focus on what you have in common rather than what separates you. The secret lies in where you put your attention. Nature has no problem accepting different species in the harmony of the whole. Focusing on differences is the curse of consciousness."

"And then humility, which is a centering act," I continued, "opens me up to other possibilities."

"You said it better than I," replied the Wizard, radiating with a sense of pleasure. "If you take a narrow perspective, you will limit your possibilities. Humility enlarges your frame of reference, which makes it easier to see all possibilities. Humility is the beginner's mind. Einstein had humility because he had a beginner's mind. With it, he could see the world as no one else had ever seen it before. Einstein was a beginner, totally unencumbered by 250 years of classical, scientific tradition. It takes strength, self-confidence, courage, and trust to open yourself to new possibilities—especially if they fly in the face of conventional wisdom.

"Your ego cannot control intuition, and it has no interest in things it cannot control. The result is a loss of intuition. That loss is too high a price to pay for control. You must learn what to control and what to allow. Life is a balance between the two."

"We're taught to control. It's very hard just to allow things to happen." I shrugged. I thought about the progression of my cancer, my not allowing the children to learn from their mistakes, and the vigil I keep over my staff at work.

"The ego does not like to allow," declared the Wizard, "yet creativity is an allowing process. You cannot control the outcome of the creative process. If you try to control its outcome, you will lose the benefits that you seek. Creativity comes with intuition, not with analysis and reason. To gain control of the creative process, you will have to surrender yourself to intuition. Your ego does not understand that.

"Surrendering to intuition is risky, but risk does have its rewards. Your five senses detect only a very limited portion of what *is*. Without intuition as a sixth sense, you would have a very incomplete understanding of what *is*."

"There's that magic word again—is." I lighted up as if I'd just seen an old friend. "I recall you saying intuition gives us access to what *is*."

"What *is* is the truth, and intuition helps you access it. Everyone is naturally intuitive, but you and most other people don't know it because your conscious mind distracts you. Your awareness increases when you quiet the noises of your conscious mind. This is the power of centering—the power of prayer, meditation, or just plain solitude. It is in these quiet moments that the truth is most likely to reveal itself, as in Major Keeble's saga.

"Intuition also tends to happen when it is least expected. After a long and passionate pursuit, having exhausted your conscious powers, you put your thoughts on the back burner. Later, in some trivial pursuit you get a flash of insight revealing answers that have eluded you in your most intense moments of rational inquiry. You need humility to allow intuition to do its work. It is a vital component to the development of the 'doctor within.'"

"The ego has difficulty with the 'doctor within.'" I spoke from experience.

"It does indeed, as the ego often cannot deal with the truth. The ego is not willing to share its turf with the doctor. Together, they could have the power of the whole."

"It's elephantine power—the power of the tusk, the trunk, and all the other parts working together," I cried exuberantly.

"Exactly," said the Wizard. "The whole is always more than the sum of its parts. In business management you often neglect the parts that cannot be measured. How do you measure staff commitment, will, spirit, purpose, teamwork, and inspiration? Is it fair to say that they do not count merely because they cannot be counted?

"Can you imagine, my friend, how much better a manager's decisions would be if she or he could see the larger whole within which they functioned? What if local decisions could be made with global considerations? The bigger scope and vision you have, the less parochial you will be with your decisions. The bigger the whole within you, the more capacity you will have to accommodate differences."

"Can you give me an example?"

The Wizard dug through his files and removed a dog-eared manila folder. He took a small piece of paper from it and handed it to me.

It read, "I have nothing, and yet I have everything—because I have God."

It was signed: *Mother Teresa.*

"Where did you get this?" I asked, completely awestruck.

"From her," the Wizard calmly replied.

I sat motionless, transfixed by the written words before me. "Where did you meet her?"

"On a flight from London to Calcutta," said the Wizard. "Mother Teresa's capacity to love is so great, she can accommodate all the world's poor. The bigger the whole within us, the more capacity we have to accommodate differences. This is the essence of tolerance. 'Bigger' people are consistently able to rise above petty differences because they are more centered and they see the larger, longer-term considerations.

"I will give you another example. The demise of communism in Eastern Europe is evidence of the power of common human longings over an imposed ideology. In his famous speech at American University, President Kennedy said, '. . . our most basic common link is that we all inhabit this small planet. We all breathe the same air. We all cherish our children's future. And we are all mortal.' That is a lovely statement of our shared commonality. If you have this truth within you, then you can absorb a lot of differences."

"Let me see if I got it. You say that truly big people are those who have a great capacity to accommodate differences because they see commonality in the larger context. And the larger the context, the smaller the differences appear to be. You're also saying that this larger context comes in part from being open to others—and this you call humility."

"Bravo!" applauded the Wizard. "This is the creative process in human interaction. It is *how to be* in life. As with all creative endeavors, the outcome is unknown— and therein lies the risk. You have to trust yourself and others to allow the creative process to happen. It is a risk because you are vulnerable. You might not get your way in the outcome. You will, however, be more likely to get an outcome which will satisfy all parties. And you will never know what other possibilities exist until you open yourself to the change process. That is humility."

"I like that—opening myself to the change process," I said. "Earlier, you told me that the role of the doctor was to open the patient to healing. The role of the teacher then is to open the student to learning. And all this is just being open to change, right?"

"It is indeed," granted the Wizard. "Life is change, and change *is* the creative process. You cannot change until you open yourself to the forces of renewal within. Humility makes this possible. You recall the first time we met, I said you have access to all the power you need within you now. When you discover it, you will have your answers.

"Mother Teresa calls this power 'God.' Havel refers to the 'higher imperative' mediated to him by his conscience. Call it what you will, it is the *ultimate whole*, the totality within which all can be assimilated. Just as water is called the universal solvent of matter, you could say your higher imperative is the universal solvent in the domain of the spirit . . . ah, I fear I have gotten a bit ahead of myself."

"You've gotten a bit theoretical," I observed.

"Then I think I will change from metaphysics to mathematics. If you wish to add mixed fractions, you have to find a common denominator. For example, you cannot add 1/2 and 1/3 until you have enlarged the denominator to six, a number common to two and three. Then 1/2 becomes 3/6 and 1/3 becomes 2/6, making a sum of 5/6. Analogously, humility is your universal common denominator. It provides a larger whole for you to assimilate differences and integrate them into a newer, larger, and more creative whole."

"I use the term 'common denominator' all the time in resolving disputes, but as always, you put a new twist on the expression," I said admiringly.

"Humility exposes you to our common humanity—the qualities of joy, love, courage, humor, and truth. Have you ever known a person with true humility?" the Wizard asked. "You can literally feel the presence of all these qualities. They are palpable. We are talking about universal qualities, qualities that are understood and valued everywhere. With true humility, the 'doctor within' has a global practice."

I leaned over the table and grabbed the Wizard's hand. "So you're saying that humility reveals what *is*—the truth, the essence of what I am. And that has universal appeal!"

"Humility reveals the commonality you share with all other people. It is a common bond of being that transcends language and ethnic differences. Right now, this common bond is obscured by different languages, customs and beliefs, and by the physical differences of size, shape, age, color, and sex. Given these explicit and visible differences, if you wish to find commonality, you must pay more attention to what is implicit about life, the invisible world of the spirit. This is the realm of a true leader. And that is the way life is."

SUGGESTIONS

Continue with your progress, as I attempted to after my meeting with the Wizard:

* THE NEXT TIME YOU MEET SOMEONE WITH WHOM YOU HAVE HAD DIFFER-
ENCES, KEEP IN MIND BEING OPEN TO CHANGE . . . AND BE CONSCIOUS OF
THE TWO PRECONDITIONS FOR HUMILITY:

  (A) SET ASIDE YOUR FIXED OPINIONS. CLEAR YOUR MIND OF ANY EXPECTA-
  TIONS, PREDISPOSITIONS, ASSUMPTIONS, OR BIASES YOU MIGHT HAVE. MAKE
  NO JUDGEMENTS. LISTEN WITH A "BEGINNER'S MIND," AS IF YOU HAD
  EVERYTHING TO LEARN.

  (B) ACCEPT THE OTHER PERSON UNCONDITIONALLY AS HAVING WORTH AND
  BEING CAPABLE OF MAKING A CONTRIBUTION TO THE WHOLE. LOOK FOR COM-
  MONALITY AND FOCUS ON THIS, ACCEPTING THE DIFFERENCES THAT EXIST OR
  LOOKING FOR WAYS THAT THE DIFFERENCES MIGHT CO-EXIST IN A LARGER
  CONTEXT, A GREATER COMMON DENOMINATOR.

* YOU MAY NEED TO SEE YOUR RELATIONSHIP WITH THIS PERSON FROM A
LONGER TIME PERSPECTIVE. BE CONSCIOUS OF ANY FIXED OPINIONS YOU
MAY HAVE THAT MIGHT BLOCK THE EXCHANGE OF IDEAS AND ENERGY.

* RECORD YOUR FEELINGS AND CONCERNS WITH THIS "HUMILITY PROCESS."
ASSESS THE OUTCOME IN THE FULLEST SENSE. SEE IF THIS ENCOUNTER SUG-
GESTS NEW THOUGHTS OR DIRECTIONS FROM YOU OR THE OTHER PARTY THAT
WERE NOT PRESENT BEFORE—IDEAS THAT MIGHT BE MORE MUTUALLY
AGREEABLE AND SATISFYING. ASSESS YOUR CONCLUSIONS NOT JUST IN THE
TRADITIONAL SENSE OF RESULTS, BUT LOOK FOR QUALITATIVE CHANGES IN
YOUR RELATIONSHIP WITH THE OTHER PERSON—ATTITUDES, ENERGY LEVEL,
BEHAVIORAL DIFFERENCES, ETC.

Leadership mobilizes the spirit of people.
Its essence is spiritual.

10

QUALITY
LEADERSHIP

The more I thought about it and the more I practiced it, I could see the power of humility. It was the foundation for openness, trust, renewal, creative interaction, change, and developing the "doctor within." It was also a prerequisite for the "beginner's mind." The gift of human consciousness, the inherent wisdom of the unconscious mind, and the pure common essence of *how to be*—all of these are related to humility.

I had read about cancer patients who considered their disease a gift because it woke them up to an appreciation of life. The Wizard and his message was my gift, but the cancer scare had also added to my appreciation of good health and the healing power of family and friends. I developed a growing sense of humility for the profound gift of life itself.

I thought about my last session with the Wizard: "I am not aware of anything unless it passes through my consciousness. Here, the ego holds sovereign sway. As with all CEOs, there are forces, like the unconscious mind, that the ego cannot control. Intuition is my window on the unconscious mind. The ego cannot summon intuition on demand, but in true bureaucratic fashion, the ego can thwart it. It can keep intuition from my awareness. This is why the ego-dragon needs a periodic bashing. It needs to learn the fine art of allowing.

"The power of humility seems to lie in its ability to reveal my true self, the *is,* that is so much a part of the Wizard's teachings. The true self is our common humanity. It is obscured, however, by our explicit differences— our languages, skin colors, customs, and creeds. For this reason, I must pay more attention to the implicit in life, the realm of the true leader." The Wizard had talked about the differences between managers and leaders before, but it appeared he wanted to take it a step further.

When I first sought out the Wizard, I found myself wanting in life. Overcome with health, family and business worries, I tried everything I could to control my life. I certainly had room for improvement—and I was not a leader. Suddenly, by becoming a "possibility seeker" some months ago, I added a whole new dimension to my problem-solving approach to life. I was ready for new insights and a new way to *be.*

When we met again, the Wizard was behind his house playing with his basset hound. He was the first to speak. "Everybody needs a basset hound. They are great stress reducers. One look at her, and all your concerns vanish."

We enjoyed a good laugh together. "I thought you were going to say that if she is that ugly and not worried, what possible concerns can we have?" I chuckled.

With his eyebrows raised and a smile on his face, the Wizard pointed to me and said, "Beauty, my friend, is in the eye of the beholder. That statement says more about you than it does about her."

"Perhaps you're right," I acknowledged.

"You left last time with a lot to think about. Is your life any different than it was before?" the Wizard asked me.

Throwing up my arms in mock helplessness, I replied,

"You tell me! You seem to know more about me than I do. I've had enough trouble coping with the visible world. Now you've got me worried about the invisible world, too!"

"Not to worry. It is all very natural, my friend," reassured the Wizard. "I merely suggested that you might pay more attention to the unseen."

"Why?" I asked, in my most childlike manner.

The Wizard paused, lowered his eyes, and stared momentarily at his hound. "In school you were taught that the world was composed of matter and energy. Yet today we know that they are one. Matter *is* energy. Everything is energy, yet did you know than nobody has ever seen pure energy? We only see the effects of it. One of its effects is matter. Matter is dense, visible energy. Your five senses make you aware of it. For most of us, matter is the only real world—it is the tangible, the visible, and the quantitative. The late David Bohm, a London physicist, called matter 'explicit energy.' In the explicit world, only matter really matters."

"Only matter matters?"

"Yes. The expression, 'It matters,' means that something is important; whereas, 'It doesn't matter,' means it is not important. In other words, non-matter is non-important. It is no wonder that our society has paid so little attention to the unseen world of energy. Our language has done us a great disservice."

"I hadn't thought of it that way," I admitted.

"Few people do, but it is time you paid more attention to non-matter. David Bohm called this 'implicit energy,' the unseen counterpart of explicit energy. It is intangible, invisible and qualitative, and it does not diminish with use or with time. When we spend it, our energy reservoir is not lessened for having done so. If anything, our energy is enhanced and others are energized, too."

"What do you mean by that?"

"My friend, if you share your happiness with another, are you the lesser for having done so? Is not the total sum of happiness greater in you and in others because of the expenditure? When you give inspiration to others, are you diminished by the amount that flows out of you?" explored the Wizard.

"When I met Mother Teresa, I was instantly struck with the contrast between her frail, weathered body and the power of her presence. Physically, she was an old woman, but the intensity and strength of her spirit lifted me. It was palpable.

"Once again, there is a language problem here. Our society has no commonly accepted vocabulary for implicit energy. Harrison Owen has written an excellent book, *Spirit,* on this very subject. Call it what you may—implicit, unseen, qualitative energy—it is simply *spirit.*"

"Can you give me a for-instance?"

"Qualitative energy, or spirit, is a state of being. Spirit is what *is.* It is about those qualities that make you one with all people. We associate it with our related humanness, with feelings like love, courage, hope, joy, laughter, and compassion. And spirit need not diminish with time. Contrast spirit with physical energy, which peaks around age twenty and then diminishes at the rate of about one percent per year. Physically, you are a diminishing asset. Spiritually, you have growth potential. Now you are a businessperson concerned with growth and the preservation of assets. Where will you put your money?" the Wizard asked me point-blank.

"That's a provocative question."

"I hope so," said the Wizard earnestly. "You have to provoke in order to attract attention to the unseen. In the competition for the hearts and minds of human beings, it is hard to compete with the material world. Matter exerts a powerful pull on our senses. We are just trying to get equal time for spirit."

"But how can we compete?" I wondered.

The Wizard invited me to walk with him. The hound led the way, her head held high, tail arcing up proudly behind, and stumpy legs padding briskly along. The Wizard, deep in reflection, said nothing. I was a little awkward with the silence. Suddenly, the basset hound stopped, catching a scent. With her ears uplifted, her nose searched the air for the scent. Then, as quickly as she had stopped, she lowered her nose to the ground and set off into the woods, barking excitedly. Moments later, she circled back to pick up the scent she had temporarily lost. Once again, her barking grew fainter as she disappeared into the woods. The Wizard paused to watch this ritual.

"Rabbit," he explained to me. Then he started to think out-loud about my question. "You asked me how spirit can compete with the world of the senses. The short answer is, with concentration, with focusing your attention, with awareness. Normally your awareness is captured by the sights and sounds outside of you or by your internal emotional reactions, such as fears or worries. You have just witnessed a classic demonstration of this. When my hound, Alphie, catches a scent, it does not matter what was on her mind the moment before. That is history! She is now totally captivated by the rabbit's scent. Her keen sense of smell regulates her life."

"But Alphie's response enables her to survive," I argued. "It isn't bad to respond to what's around you. You have to respond to the outside world, of course."

"Yes, my friend, but life for humans is more than just survival," said the Wizard. "Alphie has no choice but to follow her nose. You, however, do have choice. You do not have to follow the 'scent' wherever it goes. You have the capacity to direct your awareness to matters of your choice. Awareness takes you out of this servitude to your senses and gives you the freedom to choose. It is really the self asserting control over the senses—like a master with his hound, telling it to be still on command or sending it out on a task."

"So the issue is really control," I inferred. "Am I in charge of my mind or do I allow it to go undisciplined, randomly reacting to the scent of the moment?"

"I think you have put your finger on the key—discipline," said the Wizard. "The problem of losing focus on the world of spirit is due to the unwarranted intervention of external distractions and random thoughts. These distractions fragment you and break your concentration. You will want to be able to shut out these distractions, if you choose to do so, yet remain totally aware of everything around you. That is true concentration, the state of relaxed awareness, that we talked about earlier. If you allow your thinking process to wander around unchecked, then you will be unable to access the full power of your being."

"I've always believed that thinking and reasoning are what distinguishes us from lower forms of life," I said.

"It is true that our intellectual capacity is more highly evolved than other known forms of life, but you are presupposing that we are at the top of the great Chain of Being. Not so, my friend," declared the Wizard. "There are higher forms of life that we are not capable of understanding. Thus, faith and intuition are higher powers than thinking and reasoning."

"I see where you're coming from, Wizard. If I simply respond to stimuli, then I'm a basset hound. I want to be able to choose to 'follow my nose' rather than having my nose do all the choosing for me."

"Well said."

"Thanks. I'm reminded of our 'urgent and important'

discussion a while ago. It sounds very familiar. The hound is a slave to the urgent."

"She is enthralled and enslaved with what is urgent outside of her," said the Wizard. "The issue is how to achieve a balance in your life. In physics, they call it *equipoise* or *equilibrium*. There is no denying the material world's powerful pull on our senses."

"You said you wanted equal time for spirit," I recalled.

"Our society once had it, but sadly we have been de-mythologized. The basic theme of all mythology is an invisible or spirit world supporting the visible. The two worlds are inseparable, but we fail to 'see' the spirit. In all of us, the visible and the invisible act as one, each working its magic on the other. Our physical energy provides a fit, vital, healthy, relaxed body for the spirit. At the same time, spirit offers purpose, meaning, hope, and direction to the body." As the Wizard spoke, he cupped his hands to form a sphere. "Together they make a whole."

"I fear I'm way out of balance. There's no equipoise here!" I admitted. "With my cancer, I've been overconcerned with the physical."

"That is the norm," assured the Wizard, "but the good news is that if we admire the qualities of spirit and desire to have them ourselves, then we will move in the direction of spirit. You literally can 'absorb' from others the qualities you desire. The mental image that we desire evokes the associated feelings and actions that bring it about. See yourself as a certain kind of person, and then you will act as if it were so. There is no need not to have a balance, if you desire it."

"Then you're saying that we become more like those we admire?"

"That is right," said the Wizard. "That, my friend, is the power of leadership."

"What do you mean?" I asked, knowing the Wizard

would put a different slant on things.

"Leadership mobilizes the spirit of people. Its essence is spirit. Once again, however, language disadvantages us. For example, when ideas become tangible actions, we say they *materialize.* When leaders raise the spirit of people with purpose and inspiration, however, we do not say they *spiritualize* them. Yet, that is exactly what happens. Managers and parents mobilize material resources. In doing so, they materialize an organization or a family. They monitor the quantitative side of business and home life. Leaders, as opposed to mere managers, mobilize spirit. As such, they spiritualize an organization or a family. Their realm is the qualitative side of business and home life. Quality is the business of leadership."

"Quality and leadership are vital issues today, but I hadn't made that direct connection," I admitted.

"Much has been written about the difference between managers and leaders. I have now expressed my opinion," said the Wizard. "The manager deals with the material, the leader with the spirit. If you are to achieve a balance in your life, you need to be both a manager and a leader. The management side, like the urgent, prevails because it is quantitative. It is measurable, so you can get a handle on it. The leadership side gets neglected because it is abstract and elusive.

"This is the point: If you do not attend to the qualities of the human spirit, the quality of your products and services and family life will suffer. Quality begins with the quality of human energy expended on your products, services, and family."

"You're saying it's not the product or the service but the quality of the energy behind it all that counts," I paraphrased. "And with my children, it's not the time or the activities but the quality of energy I put into them. I suppose it's also not important to focus on my doctor's test results—it's the quality of the energy I put into my life and overall health that counts. Now *that's* a different way of viewing my life."

"You said it," approved the Wizard. "Our world cries out for attention to the qualitative dimension. This is why quality and leadership are so in demand. We have been deprived of quality because we have not acknowledged the seminal significance of the human spirit. The new frontier of quality begins with the invisible, intangible, qualitative dimensions of the human spirit: commitment, will, purpose, vision, love, and a host of others. The power of leadership grows when we share it because leaders potentiate people who release their energies and make things happen."

"And I always thought power came from control."

"It does for the manager, but not for the leader." The Wizard's manner grew more intense. "This is a very important distinction. Management power comes from *controlling* material resources. Leadership power comes from *releasing* human resources. It follows then that quality improvement starts with human considerations. This is how quality is built into a product, a service, or a relationship."

"What you're saying, Wizard, is that we build quality by building the people. That's getting people *done* through work."

"Exactly," applauded the Wizard. "Regrettably, our society is obsessed with numbers. Managers have to make their numbers, but when the numbers become the *raison d'etre,* a business loses its qualitative edge. It literally loses its spirit. What we fail to realize is that numbers are important only as measures, and they are inadequate at best. What is vital is the human energy expended to meet those numbers. Athletes know that the numbers will follow if they pursue a comprehensive training regimen that addresses the whole person— body, mind, and spirit. What works in athletic achievement holds true for business, as well."

"You're saying 'making the numbers' is important, but when it becomes my purpose, I lose sight of the human spirit, the source of those numbers?"

"Yes, and what is more," added the Wizard, "numbers are not leading indicators of how a business is doing. They are the tangible, trailing indicators. The numbers merely confirm. They quantify what has already happened. The leading indicators are all based in spirit—like hope, optimism, confidence, and courage. These are also the leading indicators of the stock market."

"Somebody once said that managing a business by the numbers is like driving a car by looking in the rear-view mirror," I remarked.

"That is an apt metaphor," said the Wizard. "You simply have to attend to the spirit if you want to be out front. There is a quantitative fixation that more is better. This is what E. F. Schumacher, author of *Small is Beautiful,* had in mind: 'The whole point is to give the idea of growth a qualitative determination.' Growth is not just more. Growth with a qualitative determination lifts, enhances, and ennobles the human spirit."

"That's what we call *quality of life.*"

"Yes, although there is some confusion there. Many who complain about a declining quality of life equate it with less purchasing power or a decrease in their standard of living. Most often, this refers to *quantity* of life. True quality of life has little to do with these measures. Most of us need a better balance, however. To achieve this, you need to remember that spirit gives life to matter. Therefore, spirit should be your first consideration."

"You're just saying I need to get my priorities right, but not neglect matter?" I looked to the Wizard for some confirmation on this.

"Of course. It is very hard to neglect matter, but it is easy to neglect spirit. That was my original point," said the Wizard. "Any way you look at the world—cosmologically, religiously, economically, historically—matter evolves from spirit. Spirit is the creative source, the producer. Matter is the product."

With that, the Wizard took a Swiss Army knife out of his pocket and handed it me. I turned it over in my hand, puzzled. "Why the knife?" I asked.

"Think of this knife as matter, crafted and sold by spirit. This product has a world-wide reputation for quality. What makes it so is the Swiss tradition of precision and craftsmanship embodied in hundreds of people who produce this product. Their loyalty, their dedication, their pride, their respect, their love—all this and much more goes into making this product what it is. If they did not feel this way about their product, their company, their co-workers, their customers and indeed, themselves, the product would lose this qualitative input, this infusion of spirit. And it would soon begin to show. So where does quality start?"

"You've made your point."

"The world is transforming in a very fundamental way," reflected the Wizard. "Matter is not what we once thought it was, and that realization is changing our material world. We think in metaphors, and as the metaphors of science change, our thinking changes with them."

"For example?"

"Throughout the industrial age, classical scientific theory, with all of its mechanical metaphors, governed our thinking. Newtonian science likened the universe to a giant clockwork mechanism. Physicists were obsessed with the search for the ultimate 'building blocks' of matter. We now know that our material world is too complex and too interdependent to be explained in mechanical terms. Quantum physics has taught us that there are no building blocks. The metaphors today are more fluid, more organic, more holistic. Physicists now talk of matter in terms of energy fields, waves, spin, velocity, and force-carrying particles. At the sub-atomic level, matter is a dynamic 'dance of energy,' and all is invisible." The Wizard opened his arms, palms up, as if to say, "Look about. It is all around us."

"As is spirit," I added.

"One in the same," declared the Wizard. "This realization of the true nature of matter as energy has been slowly sinking into our consciousness for years. With the help of the electronic computer, the symbol of the information age, this change from mechanical metaphors to energy is easier to grasp. Electronic information is pure energy."

"And so is the human spirit—pure energy," I said.

"Ironic, is it not?" The Wizard smiled. "Business, the ultimate material enterprise, is being forced to acknowledge spirit with its life-giving essence. Spirit, by nature, comes first. When you attend to spirit first, you enhance the quality of your material life. You also begin to see the larger context, the interconnectedness of life. The family is another excellent showcase for the interconnectedness of life. Acting on the basis of spirit is *how to be.*

"Intuitive people have always known that life is more than what we see. The fact is, without realizing it, we all extend far beyond the physical boundaries of our bodies and actively participate in the unseen world of spirit. This is the next frontier, and we can explore it further in our upcoming meeting, my friend. That is the way life is."

SUGGESTIONS

The "invisible world"—as if the world of matter wasn't enough to deal with now! I tried to expand my focus to a whole other realm. Here are several things the Wizard felt would help me—and you—to see how the seen and unseen interact in our everyday lives:

* LIST WHAT YOU VALUE IN A RELATIONSHIP. (HAVE A SPECIFIC PERSON IN MIND FOR EACH OF THE FOLLOWING RELATIONSHIPS.)

    WITH A FAMILY MEMBER

    WITH A FRIEND

    WITH YOUR MANAGER

    WITH AN EMPLOYEE

    WITH A CUSTOMER

  1. WHICH OF THESE THINGS ARE TANGIBLE? INTANGIBLE?

  2. DRAW SOME CONCLUSIONS FROM THIS, BASED ON WHAT YOU VALUE IN YOUR RELATIONSHIPS.

* THINK ABOUT WHAT MAKES A RELATIONSHIP DETERIORATE. HAVE A SPECIFIC PERSON IN MIND AS IN THE ABOVE SUGGESTION.

  1. ARE THE CAUSES TANGIBLE OR INTANGIBLE?

  2. HOW DOES THIS RELATE TO WHAT YOU VALUE?

* WHEN YOU ARE FEELING TIRED OR DOWN, WHAT PICKS YOU UP? FOR EXAMPLE, IT'S EARLY IN THE EVENING AND YOU'RE SITTING AT HOME. YOU FEEL TIRED AND YOU HAVE NOTHING PLANNED. THE PHONE RINGS AND A FRIEND ASKS YOU OUT ON THE SPUR OF THE MOMENT. IT SOUNDS INVITING. INSTANTLY, YOU FEEL ENERGIZED. YOUR FATIGUE IS GONE.

  1. WHAT WAS THE SOURCE OF THAT ENERGY? A VOICE? YOUR IMAGINATION?

  2. WHAT ARE YOUR REGULAR SOURCES OF ENERGY? ARE THEY FROM WITHIN YOU OR ARE THEY EXTERNAL TO YOU?

  3. CAN YOU CREATE THIS SAME ENERGY FROM WITHIN, WITH NO OUTSIDE INTERVENTION?

* THINK ABOUT AN EXPERIENCE YOU'VE HAD ON THE JOB OR AT HOME WHERE EVERYTHING WENT RIGHT FOR YOU, WHERE YOU FELT "ON TOP OF THINGS"—A PEAK EXPERIENCE.

1. DESCRIBE HOW YOU *FELT*.

2. WHAT WERE THE CONDITIONS (THE NATURE) OF THE TASK OR EXPERIENCE THAT MADE IT FEEL LIKE A PEAK EXPERIENCE?

3. HOW CAN YOU CREATE MORE OF THESE PEAK EXPERIENCES AT HOME OR ON THE JOB? WHAT CHANGES WILL YOU HAVE TO MAKE IN YOURSELF, YOUR RELATIONSHIPS, AND YOUR PHYSICAL ENVIRONMENT?

What counts is the spirit, the quality of being,
that I bring to the act of doing.

11

FROM THE HEAD
TO THE HEART

I was fearful when I went to the doctor, but the news was good—I continued to be symptom-free of cancer. This was encouraging, but in my heart I knew it would be five years before I could say I was *cured*. Knowing that I could be symptomatic at any time caused me some anxiety, but I was determined not to feel victimized. Life was too rich for me to succumb to self-pity.

As always after a visit with the Wizard, I had much to think about. He had taken the distinction between a manager and a leader a step further for me. He was now talking about spirit or qualitative energy. I had *never* talked about this, but now I saw that spirit was always implicitly present. It's true we don't give this the attention it deserves. What we see is explicit, but the Wizard said that this was only an outcome of spirit.

I had always been a number cruncher in business—and I thought I knew what it took to reach those numbers—but this whole spirit dimension was new to me. I had recently launched a quality program at work with an emphasis on products and processes. I now realized that these products were no better than the spirit that gave rise to them. The human spirit was truly the source of quality. I concluded that I had done a reasonably good job with the material side of my business, but I had undervalued the human spirit of my associates—and myself, too. I was intrigued with the idea that leaders *spiritualize* an organization. I had already seen significant changes in the spirit of my staff as I changed my behavior. But I was the leader and I had a lot more work to do on myself. I also saw how the same principles extended to my personal life, my health, and my family. I hungered for spirit to energize me in all areas of my life.

One of the most provocative things the Wizard said was that we human beings extend far beyond the boundaries of our bodies. We are inseparably linked to all about us. This unseen world is the next frontier for managers. I now appreciated the way that the Wizard liked to leave me with a teaser to think about. He also knew when I had had enough information for one time. When we met again, the Wizard was in his back yard. I asked him about Alphie.

"Oh, she is out terrorizing the rabbit world," he said. "In truth, she has never caught one yet, but that does not seem to bother her. It is the chase that excites. There is a lesson there in passion, pursuit, and persistence."

"My passion and pursuit, I fear, have been largely misdirected," I said. "I haven't been much of a leader."

"Do not be too tough on yourself," consoled the Wizard. "Few of us qualify on that count. But let me share some more thoughts on the subject.

"Qualitative energy, that which makes a true leader, can only be experienced. This is the function of art. Artists capture the ineffable qualities of life through the media of music, color, or movement. They touch our being. Storytellers come the closest. Myths are stories that symbolize the experience itself. They bring us to a level of consciousness that is spiritual. Poets use word imagery, but for most of us language is not adequate. You and I can talk about spirit, my friend, but the power lies in experiencing it."

"Perhaps we have a language for it, but it's not the language of the manager."

"Language will always be inadequate," acknowledged the Wizard, "but until we accept spirit as an equal partner with matter, we will forever undervalue its limitless potential. After all, what are the limits of integrity, will, awareness, initiative, trust, ethics, or compassion? This is the qualitative context of management. Its potential power to influence is unlimited."

"Potential power to influence—that's what it's all about, isn't it! Why didn't you say so before?"

"I thought it was apparent." The Wizard smiled at me. "I am pleased you have made the connection. Speaking of connections, you connect with others when you create and channel energy. Others feel its unseen presence which extends beyond the boundaries of our bodies. You influence others with the power of your being, with who you are. You influence them with your qualitative essence, with the magic of what *is.*"

"There's that word again!"

"It is pretty basic. Remember, when it is all said and done, is *is.*" The Wizard paused to allow that to sink in. "The point is this: When you strip away all the trappings, the pretenses, the defenses, the hang-ups, the fears, and the rationalizations, you are left with essence; and essence is pure spirit, pure qualitative energy manifested in a being . . . a human *being.* I bet you never thought about that word."

"What word?"

"Being."

"Can't say that I have," I answered with a shrug

"*Being* comes from the verb *to be,*" said the Wizard.

"We are human beings, not human *havings* or human *doings*. Hamlet said, 'To be or not to be, that is the question.' He did not say, 'To do or not to do.' Nor did he say, 'To have or not to have.' Being is a higher order than having or doing. William James said, 'Lives based on having or doing are less free than lives based on being.' Life at the being level frees you from the dependence of having and doing. You do not have to do anything. You do not have to have something. You are free to be yourself."

"I'm afraid I don't understand," I said, puzzled.

"When we talked about the placebo, I said you are free when you are not totally dependent on external things and on other people. You are free when you do not have to *have* something or . . ."

". . . or have to *do* something," I interjected. "The choice is mine at all times."

"There you have it."

"But what has this got to do with being?" I wondered. "I don't get the connection."

Alphie had returned from her hunt and was lying at her master's feet. The Wizard reached down and stroked her. The basset responded by rolling gently over to one side to expose her belly. For a minute or so, the Wizard massaged her, then he looked up at me.

"We love dogs because they *are.*"

I waited for the Wizard to complete his thought, but he was not forthcoming. I was accustomed to pauses when talking with him, but being impatient, I picked up on the Wizard's words: "Dogs are *what?*"

"They just *are.* Nothing more, my friend" said the Wizard. "Alphie is pure dog, pure being. In her world, there is no pretense, no deceit, no manipulation, no head-games, no hidden agendas, no guilt, or no hang-ups. She just *is,* and we love her for it. As a human, you complicate your life. You can learn simplicity from her. The key is to start with being."

Playfully, I asked, "Will it help if you scratch my belly, Wizard?"

He laughed and put his arm on my shoulder, pleased with the lighter side he was seeing in me. "If you'd like. That's your call. Speaking of scratching, most of us spend a lifetime scratching for a living to acquire the things we should *have* . . . in order that we can then *do* what we want . . . so that we will eventually *be* someone. As a result, we seldom achieve in a lifetime what ought to be our starting point."

"And the starting point is?" I pursued.

"Yes."

"Yes? I asked you about the starting point."

"You said, 'And the starting point is,' and I said, 'Yes' because the starting point is with *is.*"

"I should have known," I said, contritely. "You *are* the Wizard of Is."

"And *is* is a form of the verb *to be. Being* is the starting point. Inevitably you put *having* first and you put off being. As a result, you may achieve everything that is external, *having* success, but you postpone everything that is internal—*being* success. True success starts inside and works its way out. For this reason, you must start with *being.*"

"That's what you meant last time when you said I have to put spirit first?"

"Yes. A human *being* is intrinsically spiritual. We are pure spirit, encased in a mortal body. When you start with being, you begin with who you *are.* That is why you take the inner journey to find some answers to life's existential questions: Who am I? What do I want to be? Why am I here? What do I value? Knowing more about yourself, you can then make choices to *do* or *not do,* based on what you believe. When you live authentically by putting *being* first, you then *have* the quality of life you want—a life that is congruent with your innermost values and beliefs. In Havel's words, this is 'living in the truth.' Anything less than this is living a lie."

"For years I've had it all backwards, haven't I?" I said sadly. "Most people do."

The Wizard excused himself briefly and walked into the house. He returned with a well-thumbed volume of Emerson's essays. Opening it to a favorite passage, he said, "Listen to this: 'What you are . . . thunders so that I cannot hear what you say to the contrary.' Emerson is saying that what you *are* is more powerful than what you say. You feel the 'thunder' of another's being. *Being* is the context that contains your behavior. It must come first. Words and actions follow."

"This is the same power you felt with Mother Teresa, isn't it?"

"Yes, it is very strong with her, despite her age," said the Wizard. "Her being 'thunders so' that it matters little what she says. Being is not only the context for what you say and do, it is also our commonality—the community you have with others."

"Meaning?"

"We all *have* different things, and we all *do* different things, but at the being level, we are one. As human *beings,* we share the same qualities. This is our commonality with all people. When you relate at the being level, all differences of race, gender, and political preference are irrelevant. The trouble starts when you let our differences obscure our common being. This commonality of being is much greater than what sets us apart. In a major initiative to end the Cold War, President Kennedy said, '. . . let us not be blind to our differences—but let us also direct our attention to our common interests and to the means by which those differences can be resolved.' Common interests are the means to resolve differences."

"Being is the common denominator," I recalled, "that allows me to assimilate the differences of others."

"Your capacity for tolerance grows with your being," affirmed the Wizard. "The ancient Greek oracle at Delphi commanded us to 'Know Thyself.' "

"I was never certain what that meant. It seemed so self-evident," I said.

"Knowing oneself is self-awareness, a capacity unique to humans. Therefore, as you develop this capacity, you will become more fully human," explained the Wizard.

"How do I become more self-aware?"

"Once again, that is the inner journey to your being, your essence, your truth, your *is*. You will experience the real power of this journey to self-awareness when you reposition the true center of your self from your head to your *heart*."

"Do you mean to let my emotions take over?" I asked skeptically.

"No, not at all," said the Wizard. "That is a popular misconception. The word *heart,* as I use it, is much more all-encompassing. Emotions are only a piece of it. Heart is an integration or a centeredness of body, mind, and spirit. Heart is your humanness, your authentic being, your *is,* your *how to be.*"

"The real me," I said. "But doesn't the real me include my head and my intellect, too?"

"To be sure. But remember, my friend, thoughts are a lower order, a more peripheral dimension of the self."

"All right, so having recentered myself from my head to my heart, what then?"

"Then you can bring your heart, this new center of authentic human power, to everything that you say and do. And you can do it with style and individuality. You cloak your being with a mantel of words and actions to make it uniquely yours. This is what Jung called *individu-ation,* the process of becoming a true individual. It is your heart which stamps all your deeds with your seal of authenticity, because it comes from within. You are then 'living in the truth,' your truth."

"I could feel the intensity of your words," I responded humbly. "That's a pretty convincing demonstration."

"You heard the words," the Wizard corrected, "but you felt the 'thunder' of my being. For you, it was 'heart-felt.' We *do* extend far beyond the physical dimensions of our bodies, you see. The heart is the force you felt. The words are from the head. The heart is what makes you uniquely human, so you need to employ it in all your human affairs. The head is insufficient by itself. Life is larger than reason and intellect. With the heart, you are dealing with the whole of what it means to be human. Only the heart can adequately address human concerns."

"Communicating from the heart is *being.* Is that what you're saying?" I wanted to be sure.

"Right," said the Wizard. "That's what gives the heart the power to connect. Being is the container, the context in which you say and do things. When you said you could feel my words, you actually felt the context of my heart which carried those words. To feel them, however, you had to be listening with your heart. We were connecting on a being level. This is called *intimacy.*"

"Intimacy?" I showed some surprise at this.

"Yes. Intimacy is *heart talk,*" said the Wizard. "I believe we are all on a quest for intimacy, but most of us do not know how to find it. And when we do, we are often not prepared for it and we do not know what to do with it. Without the inner journey, you feel vulnerable and threatened by intimacy. That is when the ego inter-venes with its defenses to rescue you from intimacy. The ego does not know that it is rejecting the essence of life.

You need to start with *being* and that will determine your choices for *doing.*"

"You're telling me as a business manager, parent and cancer patient, that I get too caught up in doing things without attending to the spirit of what I'm doing. What counts is the spirit, the quality of being, that I bring to the act of doing. Rather than concentrate on doing, I need to focus on being. Then I can bring those qualities of being into everything I do. *Being* stamps uniqueness on all I do. Is that right?"

"You said it well," affirmed the Wizard. "The world is full of human *havings* and human *doings,* but it is rather short on human *beings.*"

My face lit up. "I love it—human havings and human doings! They certainly rule in numbers."

"Ah, but human beings rule in quality," rejoined the Wizard. "Being is the source of quality because quality begins with human qualities, with the human spirit. When we put spirit first, others experience that spirit and feel energized. This is the human connection. Experiencing another person's spirit is like breathing fresh air. Like any essence, its power lies in its purity. The more pure the exposure, the greater the impact. Pure love. Pure joy. These are the qualities that carry the messages. People put too much faith in words. We think our words will be influential. But words without the infusion of spirit are devoid of life, impotent. Conviction, commitment, sincerity, trust, joy, sensitivity—these are the qualities that give our words and deeds the power to influence. This is what sells—the invisible qualities of being, of what *is.*"

"Once again, I can feel the power of your words . . . no, of your *being,*" I said, now knowing what I felt.

"When a person you love or respect says something, it has more impact than the same words spoken by someone you do not love or respect. Love and respect are powers of the heart. In a less influential context, the words would have no power," asserted the Wizard.

Translating this into my business world, I replied, "Being 'sells.' Being adds value. It brings a quality of authenticity to any business transaction."

"Let me tell you a story, my friend," said the Wizard. "Recently I talked with a Fortune 500 manager who could 'see' his division becoming the most *respected* in his industry. This was his personal vision. To him, respect was a quality that fired him with energy and zeal. Respect was the spirit, the qualitative context within which he did business. When he shared his personal vision with his senior manager, the latter, unaware of his feelings about respect, asked him to change the word 'respected' to 'profitable.' He strongly resisted, but eventually he agreed to add 'profitable' without deleting 'respected.'

"He told me later that he was not going to let his manager remove the word from his vision. He spoke with such feeling, it was apparent that this was the source of this man's energy. Removing respect from his vision statement would have taken the vitality and purpose out of it. Generating profits did not arouse his passion. Generating respect did.

"The roots of this manager's feelings went back over a quarter of a century and tapped into the very essence of the man. His actions were flowing from the core of his being, from his heart. For him, material profits will follow when the heart is activated. To know this man was to know that respect was the source of his energy. Wise leaders know how to tap into this energy and release its power. Regrettably, this man's manager did not."

"The man in your story acted with great personal integrity," I observed.

"You have used a powerful word," said the Wizard. "*Integrity* comes from a Latin word meaning *untouched,* hence *undivided* or *whole*. When we act with integrity, we act as an undivided whole. This is what gives integrity its laser-like power. It is not fragmented nor is it fractured. It comes 'untouched' from the core of our being. We admire people who show integrity because they are being true to their inner selves. This is what Vaclav Havel meant by living openly in the 'sphere of truth.' Havel's real power lies not in his words, where he shows great mastery as a playwright, but in his integrity. This is the quality that people admire. As a leader, he thunders with integrity. He is what he says.

"In his address to the U. S. Congress, Havel said, 'The salvation of this human world lies nowhere else than in the human heart, in the human power to reflect, in human meekness, and in human responsibility.' Tell me, does this not say *how to be?*"

"He certainly says what you've been saying."

"Saying it is one thing, but taking initiative and acting on it is quite another. That is where Havel excels, and that is everyone's responsibility," said the Wizard. "It is your responsibility and it is mine. That is the way life is."

SUGGESTIONS

Try the following suggestions. See if you are more a human having or a human doing than you are a human being:

* TAKE SOME TIME TO ASSESS YOUR QUALITIES AND THOSE OF YOUR BUSINESS STAFF. BEGIN WITH YOURSELF:

  1. WHAT ARE MY SALIENT QUALITIES ? YOU MAY WISH TO ASK OTHERS FOR OPINIONS.

  2. WHICH OF THESE QUALITIES DO I FEEL PASSIONATE ABOUT? (WHAT INSPIRES ME?)

  3. DO OTHERS FEEL THIS ENERGY OF MINE AT WORK?

  4. WHAT CAN I DO TO REVEAL MORE OF "WHO I AM"? HOW CAN I LET WHAT IS TRULY ME SHOW THROUGH? (HOW CAN I LET THE *IS* SHINE?)

* GIVE THE SAME FOUR QUESTIONS TO EACH OF YOUR STAFF MEMBERS. ASK THEM TO ASSESS THEMSELVES AND PREPARE TO DISCUSS THEIR FINDINGS WITH YOU.

* NOW ASK YOURSELF THE SAME FOUR QUESTIONS ABOUT EACH OF YOUR KEY STAFF PEOPLE:

  1. WHAT ARE HIS/HER SALIENT QUALITIES?

  2. WHICH OF THESE QUALITIES DOES HE/SHE FEEL PASSIONATE ABOUT?

  3. DOES THIS ENERGY COME THROUGH IN HIS/HER RELATIONSHIPS AT WORK? IF SO, HOW DOES IT SHOW? IF NOT, WHY NOT?

  4. WHAT CAN HE/SHE DO TO REVEAL MORE OF WHO THEY ARE?

* SHARE AND DISCUSS WHAT YOU HAVE OBSERVED WITH EACH STAFF PERSON. COMPARE AND CONTRAST YOUR OBSERVATIONS ABOUT EACH OF THEM WITH THEIR THOUGHTS ABOUT THEMSELVES. TELL EACH PERSON WHAT YOU ARE TRYING TO DO FOR YOURSELF AND ASK FOR THEIR HELP. ALSO ASK WHAT YOU CAN DO, OR NOT DO, TO HELP THEM REVEAL MORE OF "WHO THEY ARE" AT WORK. THEN YOU CAN AGREE TO TAKE SPECIFIC ACTION STEPS TO RELEASE MORE OF THIS *HOW-TO-BE* ENERGY.

* REPEAT THE FOUR-STEP PROCESS OUTLINED ABOVE WITH EACH OF YOUR FAMILY MEMBERS.

If you wish to change another person's behavior,
the surest way is to change your own behavior.

12

THE PULL AND
PUSH OF LIFE

The story of the manager who wanted to make his division "the most respected" had sunk deeply into my consciousness. I wondered how often I had been guilty of imposing my ways upon my staff and my family, and I pondered the effect this had on their productivity and happiness. I discovered that when I thought about people qualitatively, I started to behave differently toward them. I was eager to talk with each of them to determine what qualities they valued and to see if they were flourishing in the work setting or at home. Then, I thought about what turned me on in life, and I concluded it was helping people develop to their best potential. I enjoyed the sense of achievement that came from helping others.

I tried to summarize what I had learned: "My essence is *spirit*. Spirit manifests itself in my being—in my heart or true self. My being is the destination of the inner journey of self-awareness because I will follow the command of the Delphic Oracle to 'Know Thyself.' *Being* is the context of all that I say and do. When I begin with being, I bring these qualities of the heart into all my choices. If I can bring being to the forefront of my life, then I will not live a life dictated by external circumstances. I will live a life which is governed by inner truths that emerge from the heart. What one *is* influences what one *does*. This is a life of integrity."

One thing troubled me, however. It had concerned me since I first heard the Wizard discuss humility—it all sounded too passive to me. After all, I was a person used to taking action, and it was not enough for me to be open to influence by others. I also needed to influence others actively. The Wizard touched on this with the power of being and integrity, but I wanted to hear more.

When we met again, the Wizard had a large map spread out on the table. He told me he was going to take a trip to the high country of Baltistan, a region of Kashmir in northern Pakistan. It is spectacularly beautiful land, and the only area in the world where three of the world's highest mountain ranges come together—the Himalayas, the Karakorams, and the Hindu Kush. When I asked him what he intended to do there, the Wizard said that he enjoyed trekking in the more remote regions. He drew inspiration from these treks. The physical demands and the majestic solitude of these locations seemed to give him a new balance, a recentering of his being. To my amazement, the Wizard told me that he would be gone for a long time.

"I am going to miss our meetings," I told him. "They have become a very important part of my life."

The Wizard smiled and, taking the compliment graciously, modestly replied, "We are an addictive society, my friend, and I think we can get addicted to anything. It is not good to be too dependent. If I were doing my job properly, you would not feel the need to continue. The 'doctor within' would feel sufficiently confident to begin its own practice."

"I think the doctor isn't through medical school yet!" I chuckled. "Perhaps it just needs a year in residency."

"Life is all the residency it needs. Your doctor will do very well, my friend. Believe me," insisted the Wizard, "it just takes practice."

"Thank you for your confidence. I needed that placebo. But when do you expect to return?"

"I do not really know. I may not," said the Wizard. "I never put a return time on these trips because I never know what will come of them. When the time comes, I will know what to do."

I was stunned. The Wizard had never indicated before that he was thinking of leaving. "You mean you may not come back to the United States?"

For the first time, I felt a slight distance in the Wizard's manner as he spoke. "There is always that possibility. You have your calling and I have mine, and we each must respond to our inner voice. I came here because I felt called to do so. My intuition tells me that I will probably be called elsewhere. But that I cannot say. I will know only when it happens."

"But what about the practice you've established, and all the friends you've made?" I asked. "And then there's the children."

"They will always be with me," said the Wizard. "As Americans, we tend to be very generous and hospitable people. Many people around the world are very fond of us and our open ways, but we tend to think that America is the *only* place to live. There are lovely people elsewhere, and we would be well advised to get to know them and their customs. We have much to learn from others. Because English is the universal language, others must make the effort to learn it. This can lead to stultifying complacency for us. We must reach out. The world needs us and we need others as well. We are all interconnected. Reaching out is a responsibility that requires initiative and patience, trust and forgiveness, compassion and discipline. It is not an easy role, but it is vital and potentially very rewarding."

"Your words are well-chosen, Wizard. Thanks for your caring advice."

"You are welcome," said the Wizard. "You have used one of my favorite words: care. You need to practice intensive care. Not the high-tech, hospital stuff, but what John Naisbitt calls the *high-touch,* human stuff."

"High-touch," I repeated. "That says it, doesn't it?"

"Yes, but it is not enough to say it," asserted the Wizard. "You must *feel* it. Intensive care comes from the heart. It has healing power. You know its presence when you feel it. When you care, any relationship is very forgiving. Actions are less important in the context of care. For example, people do not know what to say when a friend has a life-threatening illness—take your cancer, for example. In truth, it matters little what people say to you. What is important is that you know that the other person cares. A woman who lived for months with her young, dying daughter told me she learned the power of simply 'being there with love.' That is intimacy."

"That's very touching." My manner softened as I spoke. "You didn't mention the placebo, but I see it working its wondrous ways through the mother's care."

"You are absolutely right. I simply forgot to make that connection. Will you forgive me?" The Wizard smiled, knowing it was done.

"You don't even have to ask. In the context of care, forgiveness is easy."

The Wizard, allowing himself a pinch of pride, put his arm around me. "You do not need me any more. The answers that lie within seem to be emerging. You have come a long way in the times we have been together."

"Thank you." I was feeling a sense of inner composure, largely unknown to me months before. "I feel much better about myself, and it shows in my relationships. That's the test.

"There is one more thing you could help me with, however. You have been a role model for me, as I have tried to be for my family and my business associates. Many of them are action types who might see this whole *how-to-be* process as too passive. I'm afraid my influence on them will not have the impact yours has had on me."

"I thought you might feel that way," said the Wizard. "That is why I closed our last session with those few words on *initiative*. You may recall that I said it all starts within us. The whole process is dynamic and ever-changing. If I have conveyed the image of passivity, I have not been very effective."

"Perhaps I was too sweeping in my generalization," I said. "I specifically mean the emphasis on opening yourself to another's influence. How do I actively influence someone else?"

"I feel your concern," said the Wizard. "There are several factors here. First, you must remember that you cannot control others, only yourself. You cannot insure the openness of others, but you can insure your own openness. If you are open and non-defensive, you increase the chance that others will be, too. With no need to defend yourself, your energy can then be directed toward relating to others, rather than protecting yourself."

"You're saying there is power to influence others in just being open and non-defensive?"

"Spot on!" affirmed the Wizard. "You must not underestimate the power of openness. When you open yourself to another, you are giving, and giving can break through the toughest resistance. It is one of those paradoxes—in receiving another, you give of yourself. This is a placebo. It says we care."

"Actually, what I thought was a passive act is really a

powerful placebo."

"Being receptively open is vital, but you must also be *expressively* open." The Wizard's face came alive as he spoke. "If you wish to change another person's behavior, the surest way is to change your own behavior. This means doing new and different things. You are forever trying to change another without the inconvenience of having to change yourself. Changing your behavior will induce an altered response from the other person. I think this is one of the least understood truisms of home or office management.

"When you have ideas you believe to be right and good, you should advocate them *passionately*. In doing so, however, you must not be closed to others. If you recall, my objection is with fixed opinions, not opinions per se. In a relationship, the creative process demands that you merge your feelings as well as your ideas with the other person's feelings and thoughts—literally absorbing each other at the being level. In effect, the two of you become one for the moment.

"It is this creative interfusion that gives rise to new possibilities that neither of us could have imagined. I said this process was risky because you had to let go of your desire for a certain outcome. By definition, the outcome of any creative endeavor is unknown. This is also true in human interaction. You must trust the process. This is a time for simply allowing, a consciously induced 'come what may.' In effect, it is a moment of surrender to the creative process."

"Wizard, that's not an easy thing to do when we think we have all the answers. That's the ego, I guess. Generally speaking, I don't like to surrender anything to anybody," I declared.

"And that is why creativity is such a rare and highly prized quality, my friend," said the Wizard. "It is also why people have such an absence of meaningful communication at a feeling level. Ideas lead to conflict; feelings lead to commonality."

"What do you mean by that?"

"Our human condition is what we have in common," said the Wizard. "We differ in our customs, our beliefs, and our ideologies. *Communication* comes from a Latin word meaning *common*. Communication is commonality. Although we may disagree in our beliefs, we can find commonality in matters of the heart. We are all moved by compassion, inspired by truth, touched by care, heartened by hope, stirred by love, and emboldened by courage. This is the commonality of being, the irreducible is."

"This is what you meant when you said that spirit influences. These are the timeless qualities that endure, the essence that you spoke of. They speak to our common humanity, to what *is*." I suddenly sounded very much like the Wizard.

"There you are. You activated the wizard within you! Essence *is*," said the Wizard, holding up his forefinger.

"The 'wizard within.' I like that. It has alliterative power. Is that like the 'doctor within'?" I asked.

"No difference. The doctor is the wizard; the wizard the doctor. Now let us focus on your concern for action. You recall, the visualization process is linked to action. Mental imagery is an action step. We also talked about the 'cognitive receptivity' that comes with a relaxed awareness, and how you could reprogram yourself with positive images, emotions, actions, and affirmations. This is a consciously directed effort of choice.

"*Passive* implies an absence of active choice. In any situation, never say, 'I had no choice.' You *always* have a choice. The process starts with the 'pull' of awareness."

"The pull of awareness?"

"Exactly," said the Wizard. "The pull of awareness is

mindfulness, your capacity to absorb everything around you—people, ideas, feelings, ambience. You recall our discussion on centering and concentration. That process heightens your awareness and develops the 'doctor within.' This doctor makes its practice available to you. It is only this openness to all things and all people that enables you to see the multiplicity of possibilities that arise from the interconnectedness of people and events. The more connections you experience, the more options you have for action. When you look at a situation too narrowly, you diminish your chances to change it."

"Change it! That's what I mean. I have to take action to shape events and make changes. I can't just passively wait for people and events to come my way."

"You are advocating the other half of this dynamic process, the 'push' of *initiative.*" Thrusting his arm forward, the Wizard continued. "The process demands that you reach out. The push of initiative involves taking risks by getting out of your 'comfort zones,' breaking habit patterns, seeking possibilities, trying new things, being curious, exploring new facets of life, becoming adventurous, making and admitting mistakes, asking and giving forgiveness, meeting new people, changing routines, experimenting—all of these and more. Above all, it means taking initiative and being accountable for the consequences. This is an energizing process. It is aliveness, my friend."

"I can feel your aliveness," I said admiringly.

"You are experiencing what we are talking about. There is a rhythm and flow to life and its events. The creative process is all about being aware of this and knowing when and how to intervene actively to shape and direct the energy. Having sensed the possibilities that exist in a situation, you may move on any of them. *Action* naturally follows *awareness.* This is the pull and push of life. It is a natural dialogue of action, not the forced action of demands and compliance that is so unproductive. Now, my friend, does this sound too passive for you?"

"Not at all."

"Life is a mix of action and reflection, the latter being the more passive. Too much of either, however, is a life out of balance. While reflection has nothing to show for itself without action, action without reflection has little meaning or purpose. The old adage, 'The unexamined life is not worth living,' attests to the power of reflection. You need both to be complete," concluded the Wizard.

"In a broader sense, you're really talking about negotiation, aren't you?"

"Yes, but what I described runs deeper than traditional negotiation theory would care to admit."

"Everything you talk about runs deeper."

"That is the untold story, isn't it?" said the Wizard. "If you acknowledge the power of the implicit, you have to go deeper to get behind the explicit. You have to get closer to the source. That is the inner journey. That is *how to be*. To do so takes you closer to what *is*."

"It sounds as if we're back to where we started—back to what *is*," I observed.

"Did we ever leave?"

"I guess not, but you said 'closer to what *is*.' Do you think I'll ever really get there?"

"Everything hinges on awareness," maintained the Wizard. "The source of life has always been there for you to discover. In that sense, it is always available to you. In another sense, you can never hope to know fully what *is*. The 'part' cannot grasp the nature of the greater whole. In a spiritual sense, creatures can never fully fathom the nature of their Creator. A lesser power is incapable of fully comprehending the greater power.

"So perhaps you shall never know what really *is*. That

is the role of faith, hope, and trust. But you can cleanse your perceptions. In doing so, you will operate closer to the limits of your powers. You do not know those limits yet and so you must forever test and challenge them. That is what makes life such an adventure. And that, my dear friend, is the way life is."

SUGGESTIONS

The Wizard teaches balance. A "how-to-be life" is a balance between the pull of awareness and the push of initiative. Awareness is a receptive, more reflective skill. Initiative is an expressive, more action-focused skill. Most people are deficient in one or both of these dimensions. Our culture emphasizes action with its "Do something!" mentality. We pay little attention to awareness, yet this may be the most important skill you will ever learn. The key to awareness is being mindful. Many of us are so stressed-out that we lose both our mindfulness and the will to initiate. The following suggestions are designed to help you develop both awareness and initiative:

TO HELP YOU STRENGTHEN THE PULL OF AWARENESS:

* TAKE A MINDFUL WALK, PREFERABLY BAREFOOT. WALK IN A *VERY SLOW* PACE BEING MINDFUL OF THE BODY'S ACTION IN LIFTING YOUR LEGS AND PLACING THEM DOWN AGAIN. LISTEN TO THE SOUNDS AND FEEL THE SENSATIONS ON YOUR FEET. THINK OF THIS WALK AS A VERY SLOW MOVING MEDITATION WITH FULL CONCENTRATION ON YOUR MOVEMENT.

* EAT A RAISIN (OR A NUT) MINDFULLY. JON KABAT-ZINN, DIRECTOR OF THE STRESS REDUCTION CLINIC AT THE UNIVERSITY OF MASSACHUSETTS, USES THIS AS HIS FIRST MEDITATION EXERCISE. LOOK AT THE RAISIN, FEEL IT, SMELL IT, AND TASTE IT *VERY SLOWLY*. NOTE THE ACTION OF THE SALIVARY GLANDS BEFORE YOU PUT IT IN YOUR MOUTH. THE IDEA HERE IS TO BE MINDFUL OF SOMETHING WE NORMALLY DO WITHOUT THINKING.

* SCAN YOUR BODY MINDFULLY. SIT, AS IN THE RELAXATION RESPONSE, OR LIE ON A SOFT, FIRM SURFACE WITH ARMS AT YOUR SIDE, FEET SLIGHTLY APART, AND A SUPPORT UNDER YOUR HEAD. STARTING WITH YOUR FEET, FOCUS YOUR ATTENTION ON A MUSCLE GROUP AND RELEASE ANY TENSION IN IT AS YOU BREATHE OUT. PRETEND THAT ALL YOUR STRESS AND TENSION IS BEING EXPELLED WITH EACH BREATH. MOVE THROUGH YOUR BODY TAKING AS MUCH TIME AS YOU WISH. WHEN YOU FINISH, YOU WILL BE IN A MORE RELAXED AND MINDFUL STATE.

* THE RELAXATION RESPONSE, WHERE WE FOCUSED ON OUR BREATHING (IN CHAPTER SIX), IS A MINDFUL EXERCISE.

* CREATE YOUR OWN MINDFUL EXERCISES.

Mindfulness increases as you and I take a fresh approach to life. Ellen Langer's research at Harvard taught her that change requires two things: learning to think about old situations in new ways, and opening up and enlarging your frame of reference.

TO HELP YOU STRENGTHEN THE PUSH OF INITIATIVE:

* BEFORE YOU BEGIN A NEW INITIATIVE, DO A MINDFUL EXERCISE LIKE ONE OF THOSE ABOVE. THEN LOOK FOR NEW WAYS TO APPROACH YOUR SITUATION. REFRAME THE SITUATION IN A LARGER CONTEXT, LIKE A BROADER SCOPE OR A LONGER TIME SPAN. THIS WILL INCREASE YOUR OPTIONS JUST AS A NARROW PERSPECTIVE LIMITS THEM.

* TAKE ACTION, AND BE MINDFUL OF YOUR HEIGHTENED AWARENESS AND YOUR ALIVENESS.

EPILOGUE

The Wizard and I departed with embraces and great affection. He never did return to the United States, and nobody knows for certain where he went. Rumors, of course, abound. Some say he got caught in the Kashmir border conflict between India and Pakistan. Others say he is working in the devastated villages of Afghanistan. Still others believe he lives as a guru somewhere in the remote regions of neighboring China. He remains, as before, a mystery.

Curious things have happened, however. I am still coping with cancer, but my health has gained new vigor as all aspects of my life shine with being. And believe it or not, *I* have become a folk hero myself! People come from all over the world to study my business and to talk about how I achieved my success. The press has even labeled me "The Wizard of the Workplace." Sincerely, I claim no special talents. But I do say I was fortunate to learn some things from a man who taught me to consult the "doctor within."

When asked by a reporter what I had learned from this man, I replied, "In an age where everything seems to be relative, there are some enduring qualities of the human spirit. These qualities are our common humanity. They are the special qualities of being, of human being. Like the mountain massifs of Kashmir, they simply *are*. The inner journey is a quest for this source of our being, this wellspring of our humanness. It provides a rich and inexhaustible supply of energy that permeates all we have and do. It is the context of all our relationships, and it possesses enormous power to influence and to heal. It is the implicit state that surrounds all management and leadership principles, practices, and policies. It is the essence of life, the truth of human affairs, the irreducible *is*. If I have enjoyed any degree of success, it has been because I have attended to this."

With that, I said, "That is the way life is," and set out with the reporter for a brisk walk around the workplace.

✳

Selected Bibliography

Adams, John D., Ph.D., General Editor. *Transforming Work,* Miles River, 1984.

—-*Transforming Leadership.* Miles River, 1986.

Assagioli, Roberto, M.D. *The Act of Will.* Penguin, 1974.

Benson, Herbert, M.D. *Your Maximum Mind.* Times Books, 1987.

Blanchard, Kenneth, Ph.D. and Johnson, Spencer, M.D. *The One Minute Manager.* William Morrow & Co., 1981.

Campbell, Joseph with Moyers, Bill. *The Power of Myth.* Doubleday, 1988.

Chopra, Deepak, M.D. *Quantum Healing: Exploring the Frontiers of Mind/Body Medicine.* Bantam Books, 1989.

Cousins, Norman. *Anatomy of an Illness.* W. W. Norton, 1979.

—-*Head First: The Biology of Hope.* E.P. Dutton, 1989.

Csikszentmihalyi, Mihaly. *Flow: The Psychology of Optimal Experience.* Harper Perennial, 1990.

Dossey, Larry, MD. *Meaning and Medicine: A Doctor's Tales of Breakthrough and Healing.* Bantam Books, 1991.

GALWEY, TIMOTHY W. AND KRIEGEL, BOB. *THE INNER GAME OF SKIING*. PAN BOOKS, 1987.

HAMMERSCHLAG, CARL A., M.D. *THE THEFT OF THE SPIRIT: A JOURNEY TO SPIRITUAL HEALING WITH NATIVE AMERICANS*. SIMON & SCHUSTER, 1993.

HAVEL, VACLAV. *LIVING IN TRUTH*. FABER AND FABER, 1987.

JUNG, CARL G. *PSYCHOLOGICAL REFLECTIONS*. PRINCETON UNIVERSITY PRESS, 1970.

LANGER, ELLEN J. *MINDFULNESS*. ADDISON-WESLEY, 1989.

LEIDER, RICHARD J. *LIFE SKILLS: TAKING CHARGE OF YOUR PERSONAL & PROFESSIONAL GROWTH*. PFEIFFER, 1993.

LEVINE, STEPHEN. *A GRADUAL AWAKENING*. ANCHOR BOOKS/DOUBLEDAY, 1989.

MOYERS, BILL. *HEALING AND THE MIND*. DOUBLEDAY, 1993.

OWEN, HARRISON. *RIDING THE TIGER: DOING BUSINESS IN A TRANSFORMING WORLD*. ABBOTT PUBLISHING, 1991.

—*LEADERSHIP IS*. ABBOTT, 1990.

—*SPIRIT: TRANSFORMATION AND DEVELOPMENT IN ORGANIZATIONS*. ABBOTT, 1987.

PADUS, EMRIKA (*PREVENTION* EDITORS) *THE COMPLETE GUIDE TO YOUR EMOTIONS & YOUR HEALTH: NEW DIMENSIONS IN MIND/BODY HEALING*. RODALE PRESS, 1986.

PELLETIER, KENNETH R. *MIND AS HEALER, MIND AS SLAYER: A HOLISTIC APPROACH TO PREVENTING STRESS DISORDERS*. DELTA, 1977.

SCHUMACHER, E. F. *SMALL IS BEAUTIFUL*. HARPER AND ROW, 1973.

—*A GUIDE FOR THE PERPLEXED*. HARPER AND ROW, 1977.

SELYE, HANS, M.D. *STRESS WITHOUT DISTRESS*. SIGNET, 1974.

SHEALY, C. NORMAN, M.D., PH.D AND MYSS, CAROLINE M., M.A. *THE CREATION OF HEALTH: THE EMOTIONAL, PSYCHOLOGICAL, AND SPIRITUAL RESPONSES THAT PROMOTE HEALING.* STILLPOINT PUBLISHING, 1993.

SIEGEL, BERNIE S. *LOVE, MEDICINE AND MIRACLES.* HARPER AND ROW, 1986.

—-*PEACE, LOVE AND HEALING.* HARPER AND ROW, 1989.

SWIMME, BRIAN. *THE UNIVERSE IS A GREEN DRAGON: A COSMIC CREATION STORY.* BEAR & CO., 1984.

WEIL, ANDREW, M.D. *NATURAL HEALTH, NATURAL MEDICINE: A COMPREHENSIVE MANUAL FOR WELLNESS AND SELF-CARE.* HOUGHTON MIFFLIN COMPANY, 1990.

ZUKAV, GARY. *THE DANCING WU LI MASTERS: AN OVERVIEW OF THE NEW PHYSICS.* BANTAM BOOKS, 1979.

TOM THISS

The How-To-Be Book author has worked in thirty-eight countries on six continents, including a residency in London from 1983–89. Tom Thiss has taught in the business community for over thirty years, and for the past nineteen years he has managed The Ridge Consulting Group. The initiatives his firm offers to business professionals include social styles, negotiation skills, stress management, team building, adventure-based "ropes" courses, life/work planning, and a variety of organizational transformation interventions.

Tom's client list has included Aetna Life and Casualty, Bank of America, Brooks Beverage Management, General Electric, Honeywell, IBM, Kraft Food Ingredients, Minnegasco, Pillsbury, Steelcase, Texaco, 3M, USX, and Vail Associates.

He lives on one of Minnesota's celebrated 10,000 lakes with his wife Cokey, where they raised four boys who taught him his most memorable early management lessons. Tom hikes, bikes and skis, and enjoys the benefits of a regular Iyengar yoga practice. He has had a lifetime interest in health promotion and preventive medicine.

If the Wizard's words touch you in a way that you'd like to share with the author, or if you'd like to contact him for speaking engagements, you may write to:

Tom Thiss

P. O. Box 154

Excelsior, MN 55331